C-2105
ISBN 0-8373-2105-0

THE PASSBOOK® SERIES

PASSBOOKS®

FOR

CAREER OPPORTUNITIES

STATION SUPERVISOR

National Learning Corporation

212 Michael Drive, Syosset, New York 11791

(516) 921-8888

Copyright © 1992 by

National Learning Corporation

212 Michael Drive, Syosset, New York 11791
(516) 921-8888

PASSBOOK®

NOTICE

This book is *SOLELY* intended for, is sold *ONLY* to, and its use is *RESTRICTED* to *individual*, bona fide applicants or candidates who qualify by virtue of having seriously filed applications for appropriate license, certificate, professional and/or promotional advancement, higher school matriculation, scholarship, or other legitimate requirements of educational and/or governmental authorities.

This book is *NOT* intended for use, class instruction, tutoring, training, duplication, copying, reprinting, excerption, or adaptation, etc., by:

(1) Other Publishers

(2) Proprietors and/or Instructors of "Coaching" and/or Preparatory Courses

(3) Personnel and/or Training Divisions of commercial, industrial, and governmental organizations

(4) Schools, colleges, or universities and/or their departments and staffs, including teachers and other personnel

(5) Testing Agencies or Bureaus

(6) Study groups which seek by the purchase of a single volume to copy and/or duplicate and/or adapt this material for use by the group as a whole without having purchased individual volumes for each of the members of the group

(7) Et al.

Such persons would be in violation of appropriate Federal and State statutes.

PROVISION OF LICENSING AGREEMENTS. — Recognized educational commercial, industrial, and governmental institutions and organizations, and others legitimately engaged in educational pursuits, including training, testing, and measurement activities, may address a request for a licensing agreement to the copyright owners, who will determine whether, and under what conditions, including fees and charges, the materials in this book may be used by them. In other words, a licensing facility *exists* for the legitimate use of the material in this book on other than an individual basis. However, it is asseverated and affirmed here that the materials in this book *CANNOT* be used without the receipt of the express permission of such a licensing agreement from the Publishers.

NATIONAL LEARNING CORPORATION
212 Michael Drive
Syosset, New York 11791

Inquiries re licensing agreements should be addressed to:
The President
National Learning Corporation
212 Michael Drive
Syosset, New York 11791

PASSBOOK SERIES®

The *PASSBOOK SERIES*® has been created to prepare applicants and candidates for the ultimate academic battlefield – the examination room.

At some time in our lives, each and every one of us may be required to take an examination – for validation, matriculation, admission, qualification, registration, certification, or licensure.

Based on the assumption that every applicant or candidate has met the basic formal educational standards, has taken the required number of courses, and read the necessary texts, the *PASSBOOK SERIES*® furnishes the one special preparation which may assure passing with confidence, instead of failing with insecurity. **Examination questions –** together with answers – are furnished as the basic vehicle for study so that the mysteries of the examination and its compounding difficulties may be eliminated or diminished by a sure method.

This book is meant to help you pass your examination provided that you qualify and are serious in your objective.

The entire field is reviewed through the huge store of content information which is succinctly presented through a provocative and challenging approach – the question-and-answer method.

A climate of success is established by furnishing the correct answers at the end of each test.

You soon learn to recognize types of questions, forms of questions, and patterns of questioning. You may even begin to anticipate expected outcomes.

You perceive that many questions are repeated or adapted so that you gain acute insights, which may enable you to score many sure points.

You learn how to confront new questions, or types of questions, and to attack them confidently and work out the correct answers.

You note objectives and emphases, and recognize pitfalls and dangers, so that you may make positive educational adjustments.

Moreover, you are kept fully informed in relation to new concepts, methods, practices, and directions in the field.

You discover that you are actually taking the examination all the time: you are preparing for the examination by "taking" an examination, not by reading extraneous and/or supererogatory textbooks.

In short, this PASSBOOK® used directedly, should be an important factor in helping you to pass your test.

SUPERVISION, ADMINISTRATION, MANAGEMENT AND ORGANIZATION
EXAMINATION SECTION

CONTENTS

PHILOSOPHY, PRINCIPLES, PRACTICES, AND TECHNICS
OF
SUPERVISION, ADMINISTRATION, MANAGEMENT, AND ORGANIZATION
CONTENTS

CONTENTS (cont'd)

STATION SUPERVISOR

DUTIES AND RESPONSIBILITIES
To be in responsible charge of a major subdivision of the Station Department. Perform such other duties as the transit authority is authorized by law to prescribe in its regulations.

EXAMPLES OF TYPICAL TASKS
Is in charge of a major subdivision of the Station Department and the associated forces engaged in the receipt and collection of revenue, the station cleaning and the manning of station controls. Supervises and plans the assignment of station personnel. Makes inspection and takes appropriate action on condition of stations and station equipment. Prepares budgets. Evaluates equipment and materials. Plans and administers the revenue record system. Analyzes records and makes recommendations. Plans investigations and makes reports. Makes decisions involving movement of passengers during emergencies.

SCOPE OF THE EXAMINATION
The written test may include questions designed to test for: knowledge of the work procedures of subordinate employees in the Station Department and the ability to supervise them; ability to manage a major subdivision of the Station Department; ability to understand and interpret given rules and regulations and Station Department procedures; ability to conduct investigations; knowledge of job related arithmetic; knowledge of the transit authority train system and its operations; and other related items.

HOW TO TAKE A TEST

I. YOU MUST PASS AN EXAMINATION
   A. *WHAT EVERY CANDIDATE SHOULD KNOW*
      Examination applicants often ask us for help in preparing for
the written test. What can I study in advance?
What kinds of questions will be asked? How will the test be given?
How will the papers be graded?
      As an applicant for a civil service examination, you may be won-
dering about some of these things. Our purpose here is to suggest effective methods of advance study and to describe civil service examinations.
   ,   Your chances for success on this examination can be increased if
you know how to prepare. Those "pre-examination jitters" can be re-
duced if you know what to expect. You can even experience an adven-
ture in good citizenship if you know why civil service examinations
are given.
   B. *WHY ARE CIVIL SERVICE EXAMINATIONS GIVEN?*
      Civil service examinations are important to you in two ways. As
a citizen, you want public jobs filled by employees who know how to
do their work. As a job-seeker, you want a fair chance to compete for
that job on an equal footing with other candidates. The best known
means of accomplishing this two-fold goal is the competitive examination.
      Examinations are widely publicized throughout the nation. They
may be administered for jobs in federal, state, city, municipal, town,
or village governments or agencies.
      Any citizen may apply, with some limitations, such as the age or
residence of applicants. Your experience and education may be reviewed
to see whether you meet the requirements for the particular examination. When these requirements exist, they are reasonable and are applied consistently to all applicants. Thus, a competitive examination
may cause you some uneasiness now, but it is your privilege and safe-
guard.
   C. *HOW ARE CIVIL SERVICE EXAMINATIONS DEVELOPED?*
      Examinations are carefully written by trained technicians who
are specialists in the field known as "psychological measurement,"
in consultation with recognized authorities in the field of work that
the test will cover. These experts recommend the subject matter areas
or skills to be tested; only those knowledges or skills important to
your success on the job are included. The most reliable books and
source materials available are used as references. Together, the experts and technicians judge the difficulty level of the questions.
      Test technicians know how to phrase questions so that the prob-
lem is clearly stated. Their ethics do not permit "trick" or "catch"
questions. Questions may have been tried out on sample groups, or
subjected to statistical analysis, to determine their usefulness.
      Written tests are often used in combination with performance
tests, ratings of training and experience, and oral interviews. All
of these measures combine to form the best known means of finding
the right man for the right job.

II. HOW TO PASS THE WRITTEN TEST

A. NATURE OF THE EXAMINATION

To prepare intelligently for civil service examinations, you should know how they differ from school examinations you have taken. In school you were assigned certain definite pages to read or subjects to cover. The examination questions were quite detailed and usually emphasized memory. Civil service examinations, on the other hand, try to discover your present ability to perform the duties of a position, plus your potentiality to learn these duties. In other words, a civil service examination attempts to predict how successful you will be. Questions cover such a broad area that they cannot be as minute and detailed as school examination questions.

In the public service similar kinds of work, or positions, are grouped together in one "class." This process is known as "position-classification." All the positions in a class are paid according to the salary range for that class. One class title covers all these positions, and they are all tested by the same examination.

B. FOUR BASIC STEPS

1. Study the Announcement.--How, then, can you know what subjects to study? Our best answer is: "Learn as much as possible about the class of positions for which you have applied." The examination will test the knowledge, skills, and abilities needed to do the work.

Your most valuable source of information about the position you want is the official announcement of the examination. This announcement lists the training and experience qualifications. Check these standards and apply only if you come reasonably close to meeting them.

The brief description of the position in the examination announcement offers some clues to the subjects which will be tested. Think about the job itself. Review the duties in your mind. Can you perform them, or are there some in which you are rusty? Fill in the blank spots in your preparation.

Many jurisdictions preview the written test in the examination announcement by including a section called "Knowledge and Abilities Required," "Scope of Examination," or some similar heading. Here you will find out specifically what fields will be tested.

2. Review Your Own Background.-- Once you learn in general what the position is all about, and what you need to know to do the work, ask yourself which subjects you already know fairly well and which need improvement. You may wonder whether to concentrate on improving your strong areas or on building some background in your fields of weakness. When the announcement has specified "some knowledge" or "considerable knowledge," or has used adjectives such as "beginning principles of ...." or "advanced .....methods," you can get a clue as to the number and difficulty of questions to be asked in any given field. More questions, and hence broader coverage, would be included for those subjects which are more important in the work. Now weigh your strengths and weaknesses against the job requirements and prepare accordingly.

3. Determine the Level of the Position.-- Another way to tell how intensively you should prepare is to understand the level of the job for which you are applying. Is it the entering level? In other words, is this the position in which beginners in a field of work are hired? Or is it an intermediate or advanced level? Sometimes this is indicated by such words as "Junior" or "Senior" in the class title. Other jurisdictions use Roman numerals to designate the level: Clerk I,

Clerk II, for example. The word "Supervisor" sometimes appears in the title. If the level is not indicated by the title, check the description of duties. Will you be working under very close supervision, or will you have responsibility for independent decisions in this work?

4. Choose Appropriate Study Materials.-- Now that you know the subjects to be examined and the relative amount of each subject to be covered, you can choose suitable study materials. For beginning level jobs, or even advanced ones, if you have a pronounced weakness in some aspect of your training, read a modern, standard textbook in that field. Be sure it is up-to-date and has general coverage. Such books are normally available at your library, and the librarian will be glad to help you locate one. For entry level positions, questions of appropriate difficulty are chosen -- neither highly advanced questions, nor those too simple. Such questions require careful thought but not advanced training.

If the position for which you are applying is technical or advanced, you will read more advanced, specialized material. If you are already familiar with the basic principles of your field, elementary textbooks would waste your time. Concentrate on advanced textbooks and technical periodicals. Think through the concepts and review difficult problems in your field.

These are all general sources. You can get more ideas on your own initiative, following these leads. For example, training manuals and publications of the government agency which employs workers in your field can be useful, particularly for technical and professional positions. A letter or visit to the government department involved may result in more specific study suggestions, and certainly will provide you with a more definite idea of the exact nature of the position you are seeking.

III. KINDS OF TESTS

Tests are used for purposes other than measuring knowledge and ability to perform specified duties. For some positions, it is equally important to test ability to make adjustments to new situations or to profit from training. In others, basic mental abilities not dependent upon information are essential. Questions which test these things may not appear as pertinent to the duties of the position as those which test for knowledge and information. Yet they are often highly important parts of a fair examination. For very general questions, it is almost impossible to help you direct your study efforts. What we can do is to point out some of the more common of these general abilities needed in public service positions and describe some typical questions.

1. General Information

Broad, general information has been found useful for predicting job success in some kinds of work. This is tested in a variety of ways, from vocabulary lists to questions about current events. Basic background in some field of work, such as sociology or economics, may be sampled in a group of questions. Often these are principles which have become familiar to most persons through "exposure" rather than through formal training. It is difficult to advise you how to study for these questions; being alert to the world around you is our best suggestion.

2. Verbal Ability

An example of an ability needed in many positions is verbal or language ability. Verbal ability is, in brief, the ability to use and understand words. Vocabulary and grammar tests are typical measures of this ability. "Reading comprehension" or "paragraph interpretation" questions are common in many kinds of civil service tests. You are given a paragraph of written material and asked to find its central meaning.

3. Numerical Ability

Number skills can be tested by the familiar arithmetic problem, by checking paired lists of numbers to see which are alike and which are different, or by interpreting charts and graphs. In the latter test, a graph may be printed in the test booklet which you are asked to use as the basis for answering questions.

4. Observation

A popular test for law-enforcement positions is the observation test. A picture is shown to you for several minutes, then taken away. Questions about the picture test your ability to observe both details and larger elements.

5. Following Directions

In many positions in the public service, the employee must be able to carry out written instructions dependably and accurately. You may be given a chart with several columns, each column listing a variety of information. The questions require you to carry out directions involving the information given in the chart.

6. Skills and Aptitudes

Performance tests effectively measure some manual skills and aptitudes. When the skill is one in which you are trained, such as typing or shorthand, you can practice. These tests are often very much like those given in business school or high school courses. For many of the other skills and aptitudes, however, no short-time preparation can be made. Skills and abilities natural to you or that you have developed throughout your lifetime are being tested.

Many of the general questions just described provide all the data needed to answer the questions and ask you to use your reasoning ability to find the answers. Your best preparation for these tests, as well as for tests of facts and ideas, is to be at your physical and mental best. You, no doubt, have your own methods of getting into an exam-taking mood and keeping "in shape." The next section lists some ideas on this subject.

IV. KINDS OF QUESTIONS

Only rarely is the "essay" question, which you answer in narrative form, used in civil service tests. Civil service tests are usually of the short-answer type. Full instructions for answering these questions will be given to you at the examination. But in case this is your first experience with short-answer questions and separate answer sheets, here is what you need to know.

1. Multiple-Choice Questions

Most popular of the short-answer questions is the "multiple-choice" or "best-answer" question. It can be used, for example, to test for factual knowledge, ability to solve problems, or judgment in meeting situations found at work.

A multiple-choice question is normally one of three types:

(1) It can begin with an incomplete statement followed by several possible endings. You are to find the one ending which *best* completes the statement, although some of the others may not be entirely wrong.

(2) It can also be a complete statement in the form of a question which is answered by choosing one of the statements listed.

(3) It can be in the form of a problem -- again you select the best answer.

Here is an example of a multiple-choice question with a discussion which should give you some clues as to the method for choosing the right answer.

SAMPLE QUESTION:

When an employee has a complaint about his assignment, the action which will *best* help him overcome his difficulty is

    (A) to discuss his difficulty with his co-workers
    (B) to take the problem to the head of the organization
    (C) to take the problem to the person who gave him the
        assignment
    (D) to say nothing to anyone about his complaint

In answering this question you should study each of the choices to find which is best. Consider choice (A). Certainly an employee may discuss his complaint with fellow employees, but no change or improvement can result, and the complaint remains unsolved. Choice (B) is a poor choice since the head of the organization probably does not know what assignment you have been given, and taking your problem to him is known as "going over the head" of the supervisor. The supervisor, or person who made the assignment, is the person who can clarify it or correct any injustice. Choice (C) is, therefore, correct. To say nothing, as in choice (D), is unwise. Supervisors have an interest in knowing the problems employees are facing, and the employee is seeking a solution to his problem.

  2. True-False Questions

The "true-false" or "right-wrong" form of question is sometimes used. Here a complete statement is given. Your problem is to decide whether the statement is right or wrong.

SAMPLE QUESTION:

A person-to-person long distance telephone call costs less than a station-to-station call to the same city.

This question is wrong, or "false," since person-to-person calls are more expensive.

This is not a complete list of all possible question forms, although most of the others are variations of these common types. You will always get complete directions for answering questions. Be sure you understand *how* to mark your answers -- ask questions until you do.

V. RECORDING YOUR ANSWERS

For an examination with very few applicants, you may be told to record your answers in the test booklet itself. Separate answer sheets are much more common. If this separate answer sheet is to be scored by machine -- and this is often the case -- it is highly important that you mark your answers correctly in order to get credit.

An electric test-scoring machine is often used in civil service offices because of the speed with which papers can be scored. Machine-scored answer sheets must be marked with a special pencil, which will be given to you. This pencil has a high graphite content which responds to the electrical scoring machine. As a matter of fact, stray dots may register as answers, so do not let your pencil rest on the answer sheet while you are pondering the correct answer. Also, if your pencil lead breaks or is otherwise defective, ask for another.

Since the answer sheet will be dropped in a slot in the scoring machine, be careful not to bend the corners or get the paper crumpled.

The answer sheet normally has five vertical columns of numbers, with 30 numbers to a column. These numbers correspond to the question numbers in your test booklet. After each number, going across the page, are four or five pairs of dotted lines. These short dotted lines have small letters or numbers above them. The first two pairs may also have a "T" and "F" above the letters. This indicates that the first two pairs only are to be used if the questions are of the true-false type. If the questions are multiple-choice, disregard this "T" and "F" completely, and pay attention only to the small number or letters.

Answer your questions in the manner of the sample that follows. Proceed in the sequential steps outlined below.

Assume that you are answering question 32, which is:

32. The largest city in the United States is:
    A. Washington, D.C.   B. New York City   C. Chicago
    D. Detroit   E. San Francisco

1. Choose the answer you think is best.
    New York City is the largest, so choice B is correct.
2. Find the row of dotted lines numbered the same as the question you are answering.
    This is question number 32, so find row number 32.
3. Find the pair of dotted lines corresponding to the answer you have chosen.
    You have chosen answer B, so find the pair of dotted lines marked "B".
4. Make a solid black mark between the dotted lines.
    Go up and down two or three times with your pencil so plenty of graphite rubs off, but do not let the mark get outside or above the dots.

VI. BEFORE THE TEST

Common sense will help you find procedures to follow to get ready for an examination. Too many of us, however, overlook these sensible measures. Indeed, nervousness and fatigue have been found to be the most serious reasons why applicants fail to do their best on civil service tests. Here is a list of reminders.

1. Begin Your Preparation Early

   Don't wait until the last minute to go scurrying around for books and materials or to find out what the position is all about.
2. Prepare Continuously

   An hour a night for a week is better than an all-night cram session. This has been definitely established. What is more, a night a week for a month will return better dividends than crowding your study into a shorter period of time.
3. Locate the Place of the Examination

   You have been sent a notice telling you when and where to report for the examination. If the location is in a different town or otherwise unfamiliar to you, it would be well to inquire the best route and learn something about the building.
4. Relax the Night Before the Test

   Allow your mind to rest. Do not study at all that night. Plan some mild recreation or diversion; then go to bed early and get a good night's sleep.
5. Get Up Early Enough to Make a Leisurely Trip to the Place for the Test

   Then unforeseen events, traffic snarls, unfamiliar buildings, will not upset you.
6. Dress Comfortably

   A written test is not a fashion show. You will be known by number and not by name, so wear something comfortable.
7. Leave Excess Paraphernalia at Home

   Shopping bags and odd bundles will get in your way. You need bring only the items mentioned in the official notice sent to you; usually everything you need is provided. Do not bring reference books to the examination. They will only confuse those last minutes and be taken away from you when in the test room.
8. Arrive Somewhat Ahead of Time

   If because of transportation schedules you must get there very early, bring a newspaper or magazine to take your mind off yourself while waiting.
9. Locate the Examination Room

   When you have found the proper room, you will be directed to the seat or part of the room where you will sit. Sometimes you are given a sheet of instructions to read while you are waiting. Do not fill out any forms until you are told to do so; just read them and be ready.
10. Relax and Prepare to Listen to the Instructions
11. If you have any physical problem that may keep you from doing your best, be sure to tell the test administrator. If you are sick, or in poor health, you really cannot do your best on the test. You can come back and take the test some other time.

VII. AT THE TEST

The day of the test is here and you have the test booklet in your hand. The temptation to get going is very strong. Caution! There is more to success than knowing the right answers. You must know how to identify your papers and understand variations in the type of short-answer question used in this particular examination. Follow these suggestions for maximum results from your efforts:

1. Cooperate with the Monitor

The test administrator has a duty to create a situation in which you can be as much at ease as possible. He will give instructions, tell you when to begin, check to see that you are marking your answer sheet correctly. He is not there to guard you, although he will see that your competitors do not take unfair advantage. He wants to help you do your best.

2. Listen to All Instructions

Don't jump the gun! Wait until you understand all directions. In most civil service tests you get more time than you need to answer the questions. So don't get in a hurry. Read each word of instructions until you clearly understand the meaning. Study the examples. Listen to all announcements. Follow directions. Ask questions if you do not understand what to do.

3. Identify Your Papers

Civil service examinations are usually identified by number only. You will be assigned a number; you must not put your name on your test papers. Be sure to copy your number correctly. Since more than one examination may be given, copy your exact examination title.

4. Plan Your Time

Unless you are told that a test is a "speed" or "rate-of-work" test, speed itself is not usually important. Time enough to answer all the questions will be provided. But this does not mean that you have all day. An overall time limit has been set. Divide the total time (in minutes) by the number of questions to get the approximate time you have for each question.

5. Do Not Linger Over Difficult Questions

If you come across a difficult question, mark it with a paper clip (useful to have along) and come back to it when you have been through the booklet. One caution if you do this -- be sure to skip a number on your answer sheet too. Check often to be sure that you have not lost your place and that you are marking in the row numbered the same as the question you are answering.

6. Read the Questions

Be sure you know what the question asks! Many capable people are unsuccessful because they failed to *read* the questions correctly.

7. Answer All Questions

Unless you have been instructed that a penalty will be deducted for incorrect answers, it is better to guess than to omit a question.

8. Speed Tests

It is often better *not* to guess on speed tests. It has been found that on timed tests people are tempted to spend the last few seconds before time is called in marking answers at random -- without even reading them -- in the hope of picking up a few extra points. To discourage this practice, the instructions may warn you that your score will be "corrected" for guessing. That is, a penalty will be applied. The incorrect answers will be deducted from the correct ones, or some other penalty formula will be used.

9. Review Your Answers

If you finish before time is called, go back to the questions you guessed or omitted to give further thought to them. Review other answers if you have time.

10. Return Your Test Materials

    If you are ready to leave before others have finished or time is called, take *all* your materials to the monitor and leave quietly. Never take any test material with you. The monitor can discover whose papers are not complete, and taking a test booklet may be grounds for disqualification.

VIII. EXAMINATION TECHNIQUES

1. Read the *general* instructions carefully. These are usually printed on the first page of the examination booklet. As a rule, these instructions refer to the timing of the examination; the fact that you should not start work until the signal and must stop work at a signal, etc. If there are any *special* instructions, such as a choice of questions to be answered, make sure that you note this instruction carefully.

2. When you are ready to start work on the examination, that is as soon as the signal has been given, read the instructions to each question booklet, underline any key words or phrases, such as *least, best, outline, describe,* and the like. In this way you will tend to answer as requested rather than discover on reviewing your paper that you *listed without describing,* that you selected the *worst* choice rather than the *best* choice, etc.

3. If the examination is of the objective or so-called multiple-choice type, that is, each question will also give a series of possible answers: A, B, C, or D, and you are called upon to select the best answer and write the letter next to that answer on your answer paper, it is advisable to start answering each question in turn. There may be anywhere from 50 to 100 such questions in the three or four hours allotted and you can see how much time would be taken if you read through all the questions before beginning to answer any. Furthermore, if you come across a question or a group of questions which you know would be difficult to answer, it would undoubtedly affect your handling of all the other questions.

4. If the examination is of the esssay-type and contains but a few questions, it is a moot point as to whether you should read all the questions before starting to answer any one. Of course if you are given a choice, say five out of seven and the like, then it is essential to read all the questions so you can eliminate the two which are most difficult. If, however, you are asked to answer all the questions, there may be danger in trying to answer the easiest one first because you may find that you will spend too much time on it. The best technique is to answer the first question, then proceed to the second, etc.

5. Time your answers. Before the examination begins, write down the time it started, then add the time allowed for the examination and write down the time it must be completed, then divide the time available somewhat as follows:

    (a) If 3½ hours are allowed, that would be 210 minutes. If you have 80 objective-type questions, that would be an average of 2½ minutes per question. Allow yourself no more than 2 minutes per question, or a total of 160 minutes, which will permit about 50 minutes to review.

    (b) If for the time allotment of 210 minutes, there are 7 essay questions to answer, that would average about 30 minutes a question. Give yourself only 25 minutes per question so that you have about 35 minutes to review.

6. The most important instruction is *to read each question* and make sure you know what is wanted. The second most important instruction is to *time yourself properly* so that you answer every question. The third most important instruction is to *answer every question*. Guess if you have to but include something for each question. Remember that you will receive no credit for a blank and will probably receive some credit if you write something in answer to an essay question. If you guess a letter, say "B" for a multiple-choice question, you may have guessed right. If you leave a blank as the answer to a multiple-choice question, the examiners may respect your feelings but it will not add a point to your score.

7. Suggestions

    a. <u>Objective-Type Questions</u>

        (1) Examine the question booklet for proper sequence of pages and questions.

        (2) Read all instructions carefully.

        (3) Skip any question which seems too difficult; return to it after all other questions have been answered.

        (4) Apportion your time properly; do not spend too much time on any single question or group of questions.

        (5) Note and underline key words -- *all, most, fewest, least, best, worst, same, opposite.*

        (6) Pay particular attention to negatives.

        (7) Note unusual option, e.g., unduly long, short, complex, different or similar in content to the body of the question.

        (8) Observe the use of "hedging" words -- *probably, may, most likely, etc.*

        (9) Make sure that your answer is put next to the same number as the question.

       (10) Do not second-guess unless you have good reason to believe the second answer is definitely more correct.

       (11) Cross out original answer if you decide another answer is more accurate; do not erase.

       (12) Answer all questions; guess unless instructed otherwise.

       (13) Leave time for review.

    b. <u>Essay-Type Questions</u>

        (1) Read each question carefully.

        (2) Determine exactly what is wanted. Underline key words or phrases.

        (3) Decide on outline or paragraph answer.

        (4) Include many different points and elements unless asked to develop any one or two points or elements.

        (5) Show impartiality by giving pros and cons unless directed to select one side only.

        (6) Make and write down any assumptions you find necessary to answer the question.

        (7) Watch your English, grammar, punctuation, choice of words.

        (8) Time your answers; don't crowd material.

8. Answering the Essay Question

    Most essay questions can be answered by framing the specific response around several key words or ideas. Here are a few such key words or ideas:

M's: manpower, materials, methods, money, management;
P's: purpose, program, policy, plan, procedure, practice,
problems, pitfalls, personnel, public relations.
a. Six Basic Steps in Handling Problems:
(1) Preliminary plan and background development
(2) Collect information, data and facts
(3) Analyze and interpret information, data and facts
(4) Analyze and develop solutions as well as make recommendations
(5) Prepare report and sell recommendations
(6) Install recommendations and follow up effectiveness
b. Pitfalls to Avoid
(1) *Taking things for granted*
A statement of the situation does not necessarily imply that each of the elements is necessarily true; for example, a complaint may be invalid and biased so that all that can be taken for granted is that a complaint has been registered.
(2) *Considering only one side of a situation*
Wherever possible, indicate several alternatives and then point out the reasons you selected the best one.
(3) *Failing to indicate follow-up*
Whenever your answer indicates action on your part, make certain that you will take proper follow-up action to see how successful your recommendations, procedures, or actions turn out to be.
(4) *Taking too long in answering any single question*
Remember to time your answers properly.

IX. AFTER THE TEST

Scoring procedures differ in detail among civil service jurisdictions although the general principles are the same. Whether the papers are hand-scored or graded by the electric scoring machine we have described, they are nearly always graded by number. That is, the person who marks the paper knows only the number -- never the name -- of the applicant. Not until all the papers have been graded will they be matched with names. If other tests, such as training and experience or oral interview ratings have been given, scores will be combined. Different parts of the examination usually have different weights. For example, the written test might count 60 percent of the final grade, and a rating of training and experience 40 percent. In many jurisdictions, veterans will have a certain number of points added to their grades.

After the final grade has been determined, the names are placed in grade order and an eligible list is established. There are various methods for resolving ties between those who get the same final grade: probably the most common is to place first the name of the person whose application was received first. Job offers are made from the eligible list in the order the names appear on it.

You will be notified of your grade and your rank order as soon as all these computations have been made. This will be done as rapidly as possible.

People who are found to meet the requirements in the announcement are called "eligibles." Their names are put on a list of eligibles. An eligible's chances of getting a job depend on how high he stands on this list and how fast agencies are filling jobs from the list.

When a job is to be filled from a list of eligibles, the agency asks for the names of people on the list of eligibles for that job.

When the civil service commission receives this request, it sends to the agency the names of the three people highest on the list. Or, if the job to be filled has specialized requirements, the office sends the agency, from the general list, the names of the top three persons who meet those requirements.

The appointing officer makes a choice from among the three people whose names were sent to him. If the selected person accepts the appointment, the names of the others are put back on the list to be considered for future openings.

That is the rule in hiring from all kinds of eligible lists, whether they are for typist, carpenter, chemist, or something else. For every vacancy, the appointing officer has his choice of any one of the top three eligibles on the list. This explains why the person whose name is on top of the list sometimes does not get an appointment when some of the persons lower on the list do. If the appointing officer chooses the No.2 or No.3 eligible, the No.1 eligible does not get a job at once, but stays on the list until he is appointed or the list is terminated.

X. HOW TO PASS THE INTERVIEW TEST

The examination for which you applied requires an oral interview test. You have already taken the written test and you are now being called for the interview test -- the final part of the formal examination.

You may think that it is not possible to prepare for an interview test and that there are no procedures to follow during an interview.

Our purpose is to point out some things you can do in advance that will help you and some good rules to follow and pitfalls to avoid while you are being interviewed.

A. WHAT IS AN INTERVIEW SUPPOSED TO TEST?

The written examination is designed to test the technical knowledge and competence of the candidate; the oral is designed to evaluate intangible qualities, not readily measured otherwise, and to establish a list showing the relative fitness of each candidate, *as measured against his competitors,* for the position sought. Scoring is not on the basis of "right" or "wrong," but on a sliding scale of values ranging from "not passable" to "outstanding." As a matter of fact, it is possible to achieve a relatively low score without a single "incorrect" answer because of evident weakness in the qualities being measured,

Occasionally, an examination may consist entirely of an oral test -- either an individual or a group oral. In such cases, information is sought concerning the technical knowledges and abilities of the candidate, since there has been no written examination for this purpose. More commonly, however, an oral test is used to supplement a written examination.

B. WHO CONDUCTS INTERVIEWS?

The composition of oral boards varies among different jurisdictions. In nearly all, a representative of the personnel department serves as chairman. One of the members of the board may be a representative of the department in which the candidate would work. In some cases, "outside experts" are used, and frequently a business man or some other representative of the general public is asked to serve. Labor and management or other special groups may be represented. The aim is to secure the services of experts in the appropriate field.

However the board is composed, it is a good idea (and not at all improper or unethical) to ascertain in advance of the interview who the members are and what groups they represent. When you are introduced to them, you will have some idea of their backgrounds and interests, and at least you will not stutter and stammer over their names.

C. *WHAT TO DO BEFORE THE INTERVIEW*

While knowledge about the board members is useful and takes some of the surprise element out of the interview, there is other preparation which is more substantive. It *is* possible to prepare for an oral -- in several ways:

1. Keep a Copy of Your Application and Review it Carefully Before the Interview

    This may be the only document before the oral board, and the starting point of the interview. Know what experience and education you have listed there, and the sequence and dates of it. Sometimes the board will ask *you* to review the highlights of your experience for them; you should not have to hem and haw doing it.

2. Study the Class Specification and the Examination Announcement

    Usually, the oral board has one or both of these to guide them. The qualities, characteristics, or knowledges required by the position sought are stated in these documents. They offer valuable clues as to the nature of the oral interview. For example, if the job involves supervisory responsibilities, the announcement will usually indicate that knowledge of modern supervisory methods and the qualifications of the candidate as a supervisor will be tested. If so, you can expect such questions, frequently in the form of a hypothetical situation which you are expected to solve. *Never* go into an oral without knowledge of the duties and responsibilities of the job you seek.

3. Think Through Each Qualification Required

    Try to visualize the kind of questions *you* would ask if you were a board member. How well could you answer them? Try especially to appraise your own knowledge and background in each area, *measured against the job sought,* and identify any areas in which you are weak. Be critical and realistic -- do not flatter yourself.

4. Do Some General Reading in Areas in Which You Feel You May be Weak

    For example, if the job involves supervision and your past experience has *not,* some general reading in supervisory methods and practices, particularly in the field of human relations, might be useful. *Do not* study agency procedures or detailed manuals. The oral board will be testing your understanding and capacity, *not* your memory.

5. Get a Good Night's Sleep and Watch Your General Health and Mental Attitude

    You will want a clear head at the interview. Take care of a cold or other minor ailment, and, of course, *no hangovers.*

13

D. WHAT TO DO THE DAY OF THE INTERVIEW

Now comes the day of the interview itself. Give yourself plenty of time to get there. Plan to arrive somewhat ahead of the scheduled time, particularly if your appointment is in the fore part of the day. If a previous candidate fails to appear, the board might be ready for you a bit early. By early afternoon an oral board is almost invariably behind schedule if there are many candidates, and you may have to wait. Take along a book or magazine to read, or your application to review. But leave any extraneous material in the waiting room when you go in for your interview. In any event, relax and compose yourself.

The matter of dress is important. The board is forming impressions about you -- from your experience, your manners, your attitudes, and from your appearance. Give your personal appearance careful attention. Dress your *best*, but not your flashiest. Choose conservative, appropriate clothing, and be sure it and you are immaculate. This is a business interview, and your appearance should indicate that you regard it as such. Besides, being well-groomed and properly dressed will help boost your confidence.

Sooner or later, someone will call your name and escort you into the interview room. *This is it.* From here on you are on your own. It is too late for any more preparation. But, remember, you asked for this opportunity to prove your fitness, and you are here because your request was granted.

E. WHAT HAPPENS WHEN YOU GO IN?

The usual sequence of events will be as follows: The clerk (who is often the board stenographer) will introduce you to the chairman of the oral board, who will introduce you to each other member of the board. Acknowledge the introductions before you sit down. Do not be surprised if you find a microphone facing you or a stenotypist sitting by. Oral interviews are usually recorded, in the event of an appeal or other review.

Usually the chairman of the board will open the interview by reviewing the highlights of your education and work experience from your application -- primarily for the benefit of the other members of the board, as well as to get the material into the record. Do not interrupt or comment unless there is an error or significant misinterpretation; if so, do not hesitate. But do not quibble about insignificant matters. Usually, also, he will ask you some question about your education, your experience, or your present job -- partly to get you started talking, to establish the interviewing "rapport." He may start the actual questioning, or turn it over to one of the other members. Frequently each member undertakes the questioning on a particular area, one in which he is perhaps most competent. So you can expect each member to participate in the examination. And because the time is limited, you may expect some rather abrupt switches in the direction the questioning takes. Do not be upset by it. Normally, a board member will not pursue a single line of questioning unless he discovers a particular strength or weakness.

After each member has participated, the chairman will usually ask whether any member has any further questions, then will ask you if you have anything you wish to add. Unless you are expecting this question, it may floor you. Or worse, it may start you off on an extended, extemporaneous speech. The board is not usually seeking more information. The question is principally to offer you a last opportunity to present further qualifications or to indicate that you have nothing to add. So, if you feel that a significant qualification or characteristic has been overlooked, it is proper to point it out in a sentence or so. Do not compliment the board on the thoroughness of their examination -- they have been sketchy, and you know it. If you wish, merely say, "No thank you, I have nothing further to add." This is a point where you can "talk yourself out" of a good impression or fail to present an important bit of information. *Remember, you close the interview yourself*.

The chairman will then say,"That is all,Mr.Smith,thank you." Do not be startled; the interview is over, and quicker than you think. Say,"Thank you and good morning," gather up your belongings and take your leave. Save your sigh of relief for the other side of the door.

F. *HOW TO PUT YOUR BEST FOOT FORWARD*

Throughout all this process, you may feel that the board individually and collectively is trying to pierce your defenses, to seek out your hidden weaknesses, and to embarrass and confuse you. Actually, this is not true. They are obliged to make an appraisal of your qualifications for the job you are seeking, and they *want to see you in your best light*. Remember, they must interview all candidates and a noncooperative candidate may become a failure in spite of their best efforts to bring out his qualifications. Here are fifteen(15) suggestions that will help you:

1. Be Natural. Keep Your Attitude Confident,But Not Cocky

If *you* are not confident that you can do the job, do not expect the *board* to be. Do not apologize for your weaknesses, try to bring out your strong points. The board is interested in a positive, not a negative presentation. Cockiness will antagonize any board member, and make him wonder if you are covering up a weakness by a false show of strength.

2. Get Comfortable, But Don't Lounge or Sprawl

Sit erectly but not stiffly. A careless posture may lead the board to conclude you are careless in other things, or at least that you are not impressed by the importance of the occasion to you.Either conclusion is natural, even if incorrect. Do not fuss with your clothing, or with a pencil or an ashtray. Your hands may occasionally be useful to emphasize a point; do not let them become a point of distraction.

3. Do Not Wisecrack or Make Small Talk

This is a serious situation, and your attitude should show that you consider it as such. Further, the time of the board is limited; they do not want to waste it, and neither should you.

4. Do Not Exaggerate Your Experience or Abilities

In the first place, from information in the application,from other interviews and other sources, the board may know more about you than you think; in the second place, you probably will not get away with it in the first place. An experienced board is rather adept at spotting such a situation. Do not take the chance.

5. If You Know a Member of the Board, Do Not Make a Point of It, Yet Do Not Hide It.

Certainly you are not fooling him, and probably not the other members of the board. Do not try to take advantage of your acquaintanceship -- it will probably do you little good.

6. Do Not Dominate the Interview

Let the board do that. They will give you the clues -- do not assume that you have to do all the talking. Realize that the board has a number of questions to ask you, and do not try to take up all the interview time by showing off your extensive knowledge of the answer to the first one.

7. Be Attentive

You only have twenty minutes or so, and you should keep your attention at its sharpest throughout. When a member is addressing a problem or a question to you, give him your undivided attention. Address your reply principally to him, but do not exclude the other members of the board.

8. Do Not Interrupt

A board member may be stating a problem for you to analyze. He will ask you a question when the time comes. Let him state the problem, and wait for the question.

9. Make Sure You Understand the Question

Do not try to answer until you are sure what the question is. If it is not clear, restate it in your own words or ask the board member to clarify it for you. But do not haggle about minor elements.

10. Reply Promptly But Not Hastily

A common entry on oral board rating sheets is "candidate responded readily," or "candidate hesitated in replies." Respond as promptly and quickly as you can, but do not jump to a hasty, ill-considered answer.

11. Do Not Be Peremptory in Your Answers

A brief answer is proper -- but do not fire your answer back. That is a losing game from your point of view. The board member can probably ask questions much faster than you can answer them.

12. Do Not Try To Create the Answer You Think the Board Member Wants

He is interested in what kind of mind you have and how it works -- not in playing games. Furthermore, he can usually spot this practice and will usually grade you down on it.

13. Do Not Switch Sides in Your Reply Merely to Agree With a Board Member

Frequently, a member will take a contrary position merely to draw you out and to see if you are willing and able to defend your point of view. Do not start a debate, yet do not surrender a good position. If a position is worth taking, it is worth defending.

14. Do Not Be Afraid to Admit an Error in Judgment if You Are Shown to Be Wrong

The board knows that you are forced to reply without any opportunity for careful consideration. Your answer may be demonstrably wrong. If so, admit it and get on with the interview.

15. Do Not Dwell at Length on Your Present Job

The opening question may relate to your present assignment. Answer the question but do not go into an extended discussion. You are being examined for a *new* job, not your present one. As a matter of fact, try to phrase *all* your answers in terms of the job for which you are being examined.

G. BASIS OF RATING

Probably you will forget most of these "do's" and "don'ts" when you walk into the oral interview room. Even remembering them all will not insure you a passing grade. Perhaps you did not have the qualifications in the first place. But remembering them *will* help you to put your best foot forward, without treading on the toes of the board members.

Rumor and popular opinion to the contrary notwithstanding, an oral board wants you to make the best appearance possible. They know you are under pressure -- but they also want to see how you respond to it as a guide to what your reaction would be under the pressures of the job you seek. They will be influenced by the degree of poise you display, the personal traits you show, and the manner in which you respond.

EXAMINATION SECTION

EXAMINATION SECTION
TEST 1

DIRECTIONS: Each question or incomplete statement is followed by several suggested answers or completions. Select the one that *BEST* answers the question or completes the statement. *PRINT THE LETTER OF THE CORRECT ANSWER IN THE SPACE AT THE RIGHT.*

1. A vandal throws a stone and injures a railroad porter who 1.___ is working at an elevated train station. When the porter's assistant station supervisor submits a supervisory accident report for the accident to his supervisor for approval, the latter should make sure that the proper category for "RESPONSIBILITY" has been checked off.

   The proper "RESPONSIBILITY" category that should be checked for this accident is
   A. Control of Other Than Company or Employee
   B. Impractical to Control
   C. Supervision
   D. Employee

2. Assume that you are a station supervisor and you notice 2.___ that the accident rate for a particular heavy duty cleaning gang has increased to an unacceptable level. Of the following, the *BEST* method of handling this problem is to tell the assistant station supervisor in charge of this gang
   A. to watch his men more closely when they work and to correct any unsafe work habits they may have
   B. that the accident rate for his gang is too high and that it reflects poorly on the work record of his gang
   C. that he must severely penalize those men who are most accident prone in order to set an example for the others in the gang
   D. to assign the easiest work tasks to those men who have the most accidents

3. Assume that your superior gives you orders to carry out 3.___ a special assignment. However, you believe there is an error in his orders.

   Which one of the following statements *BEST* describes the action you should take in this situation?
   A. Carry out the orders exactly as given to you
   B. Carry out the orders, but modify them to correct the error
   C. Delay carrying out the orders and give your superior a chance to detect the error himself
   D. Point out the error to your superior before carrying out the orders

4. A work sheet for a booth audit has the readings shown   4.___
below for four turnstiles:

Turnstile No.	Opening Readings	Readings For Audit
1	26178	26291
2	65489	65752
3	72267	72312
4	45965	46199

With a fare of 50 cents, what is the cash value of the
total difference between the Opening Readings and the
Readings for Audit for the four turnstiles?
    A. $317.50   B. $326.50   C. $327.50   D. $337.50

5. When an employee is suspected of being under the influ-   5.___
ence of alcohol, a member of supervision must make out
a written report of the incident. This supervisor should
include in his report the answer to certain questions
that he has asked the employee.

Following are *four* possible questions that the supervisor
might ask the employee:
   I. What kind of beverage did you drink?
  II. How much alcohol did the beverage contain?
 III. When did you drink this beverage?
  IV. How much of the beverage did you drink?

Which *one* of the following choices lists *only* those of
the above questions that must be asked for the preparation of the written report?
    A. I, II and III   B. I, III and IV
    C. I, II and IV   D. II, III and IV

6. Following are *four* statements relating to collection   6.___
train operations, which may or may not be correct:
   I. The assistant station supervisor in charge of a
      collection train must follow the prepared schedule
      of revenue collections at all times and is not
      authorized to deviate from it.
  II. The checking of bags delivered to the collection
      train will be done after the count of bags to the
      tally clerks has been completed, and while the train
      is moving from one station to another.
 III. The tally clerk will arrange the railroad clerks'
      daily reports in booth and trick order, and he will
      personally deliver these reports to the representa-
      tive of the revenue department on duty in the revenue
      room.
  IV. The tally clerk of each revenue train will check keys,
      dials and related equipment received from collection
      parties, and will see to the disposition of these
      items according to scheduled procedure, unless other-
      wise directed by an authorized supervisor.

Which of the following choices lists *all* the above statements that are correct and *none* that is incorrect?
    A. I and II   B. I, II and III
    C. II, III and IV   D. III and IV

Questions 7 - 10.

DIRECTIONS: Questions 7 to 10 require computing basic schedule
working time for certain specified tasks for porters
assigned to one station. The questions apply to an
average station for which the statistics are as
follows:

STATION STATISTICS

Tile: 3,747 linear feet (average height of 9½ feet)

No. of Entrance Stairways: 7

No. of Rolled Platform Columns: Northbound 72,
Southbound 76

Active Floor Area: Northbound Platform 12,345 sq. ft.
Southbound Platform 12,987 sq. ft.

7. The total computed time required to sweep all the   7.___
entrance stairways daily from Monday through Friday
is, *most nearly*,
    A. 1 hour   B. 4 3/4 hours
    C. 5 1/2 hours   D. 6 hours

8. If all the columns in the station must be cleaned once   8.___
in a period of 4 weeks, the total computed time that
should be allotted to the cleaning of columns each week
is, *most nearly*,
    A. 6 1/4 hours   B. 7 1/4 hours
    C. 8 hours   D. 10 1/4 hours

9. The total weekly computed time for sweeping the active   9.___
floor area twice a week is, *most nearly*,
    A. 4 1/2 hours   B. 6 hours
    C. 8 3/4 hours   D. 9 1/4 hours

10. As a major duty, the tile must be cleaned once in a   10.___
period of 4 weeks. Therefore, the total computed time
for cleaning tile each week is closest to
    A. 18.7 hours   B. 23.4 hours
    C. 27.2 hours   D. 93.6 hours

11. Assume that a new procedure affecting railroad clerks   11.___
is to be put into operation immediately. At a staff
conference attended by station supervisors and the
chief of operations concerning this new procedure, you
had objected to it because you believed it would cause
a reduction in efficiency, and you thought the present
procedure was adequate.

Of the following, the *BEST* course of action for you to
take should be to instruct your subordinates to

A. follow the new procedure, but indicate to them
   that you do not like it
B. follow the procedure which they think is best
C. avoid following the new procedure until the next
   scheduled staff conference
D. follow the new procedure and maintain careful
   notes on how it works

12. Following are *four* statements relating to procedures for   12.___
    unusual occurrences and the preparation of related re-
    ports, which may or may not be correct:
    I. At all times a prompt report of every unusual oc-
       currence should be made by telephone to the field
       office.
    II. The telephone report of the occurrence should in-
        clude the time, the place, and a concise statement
        of the circumstances and action taken, including the
        names and addresses of passengers and the names and
        badge numbers of employees and police officers in-
        volved.
    III. If the occurrence is of an emergency nature, the
         field office should be notified first and the police
         office and station department office notified after-
         wards.
    IV. Train whistle signals for help, which consist of one
        short-one long-one short-one long blast, should be
        given immediate response by station department em-
        ployees.

    Which of the following choices lists *all* of the above
    statements that are correct and *none* that is incorrect?
      A. I and II   B. II   C. III   D. III and IV

13. Following are *four* statements relating to the duties of   13.___
    collecting agents, which may or may not be correct:
    I. A collecting agent may not reveal a safe combina-
       tion except if he has received a verbal order to
       do so by the assistant general superintendent or
       his authorized representative.
    II. Unless specifically excused, each collecting agent
        while on duty will wear his uniform cap and badge
        and will also carry his revolver permit on his per-
        son.
    III. Revolvers will be issued to collecting agents in the
         presence of either the transit patrolman or the as-
         sistant station supervisor in charge of revenue col-
         lections at designated points and returned in the
         same manner.
    IV. No collecting agent should have his revolver or badge
        in his possession while off duty.

    Which one of the following choices lists *all* of the above
    statements that are correct and *none* that is incorrect?
      A. I and II   B. II and III
      C. II and IV   D. III and IV

14. Following are *four* statements relating to time card   14.___
    rules, which may or may not be correct:
     I. The entering of time worked by one employee on
        another employee's time card is forbidden.
    II. Assistant station supervisors are authorized to
        make notations on employees' time cards in order
        to draw the attention of the timekeeper to incor-
        rect entries.
   III. Time cards for court attendance and trial board
        hearings should be forwarded to the station depart-
        ment office for verification and signature.
    IV. Per annum employees are required to submit their
        time cards at designated locations on the last day
        of each bi-weekly pay period.

    Which one of the following choices lists *all* of the above
    statements that are correct and *none* that is incorrect?
       A. I, II, and III   B. I, III, and IV
       C. I, II, III, and IV   D. II, III, and IV

15. As a rule, the stairs at all stations are numbered con-   15.___
    secutively beginning at the
       A. southeast end   B. southwest end
       C. northeast end   D. northwest end

16. The type of construction *generally* used for sliding   16.___
    gates at stations is designated as
       A. "E" rail   B. "F" rail   C. "G" rail   D. "H" rail

17. At 9:00 A.M. you are requested by your superior to in-   17.___
    vestigate a situation which has arisen. Turnstiles at
    a certain station have been repeatedly vandalized over
    the past week causing a serious revenue loss to the
    authority and inconvenience to the public. You are
    told that this is an urgent job and that you must sub-
    mit a written report to your superior by 5:00 P.M. of
    that day.

    For the report to be of *GREATEST* immediate value to your
    superior, it should contain some of the following items:
     I. A brief statement of the problem
    II. A detailed description of the problem
   III. Detailed plans of the platform and station layout
    IV. An outline of possible practical alternate solutions
     V. Your recommended solution

    Which of the following choices lists *only* those of the
    above items to be included in the report so that the
    report is of *GREATEST* immediate value to your superior?
       A. I, III, and IV   B. I, III, and V
       C. I, IV, and V   D. II, III, and V

Questions 18 - 20.

DIRECTIONS: Questions 18 to 20 are based on the article shown below
              entitled "EMPLOYEE NEEDS." Refer to this article when
              answering these questions.

EMPLOYEE NEEDS

The greatest waste in industry and in government may be that of human resources. This waste usually derives not from employees' unwillingness or inability, but from management's ineptness to meet the maintenance and motivational needs of employees. Maintenance needs refer to such needs as providing employees with safe places to work, written work rules, job security, adequate salary, employer sponsored social activities, and with knowledge of their role in the over-all framework of the organization. However, of greatest significance to employees are the motivational needs of job growth, achievement, responsibility and recognition.

Although employee dissatisfaction may stem from either poor maintenance or poor motivation factors, the outward manifestation of the dissatisfaction may be very much alike, i.e. negativism, complaints, deterioration of performance, and so forth. The improvement in the lighting of an employee's work area or raising his level of pay won't do much good if the source of the dissatisfaction is the absence of a meaningful assignment. By the same token, if an employee is dissatisfied with what he considers inequitable pay, the introduction of additional challenge in his work may simply make matters worse.

It is relatively easy for an employee to express frustration by complaining about pay, wash room conditions, fringe benefits and so forth; but most people cannot easily express resentment in terms of the more abstract concepts concerning job growth, responsibility, and achievement.

It would be wrong to assume that there is no interaction between maintenance and motivational needs of employees. For example, conditions of high motivation often overshadow poor maintenance conditions. If an organization is in a period of strong growth and expansion, opportunities for job growth, responsibility, recognition and achievement are usually abundant, but the rapid growth may have outrun the upkeep of maintenance factors. In this situation, motivation may be high, but only if employees recognize the poor maintenance conditions as unavoidable and temporary. The subordination of maintenance factors cannot go on indefinitely, even with the highest motivation.

Both maintenance and motivation factors influence the behavior of all employees, but employees are not identical and, furthermore, the needs of any individual do not remain constant. However, a broad distinction can be made between employees who have a basic orientation toward maintenance factors and those with greater sensitivity toward motivation factors.

A highly maintenance-oriented individual, preoccupied with the factors peripheral to his job rather than the job itself, is more concerned with comfort than challenge. He does not get deeply involved with his work but does with the condition of his work area, toilet facilities and his time for going to lunch. By contrast, a strongly motivation-oriented employee is usually relatively indifferent to his surroundings and is caught up in the pursuit of work goals.

Fortunately, there are few people who are either exclusively maintenance-oriented or purely motivation-oriented. The former would be deadwood in an organization, while the latter might trample on those around him in his pursuit to achieve his goals.

18. With respect to employee motivational and maintenance   18.___
    needs, the management policies of an organization which
    is growing rapidly will probably result
    A. more in meeting motivational needs rather than
       maintenance needs
    B. more in meeting maintenance needs rather than
       motivational needs
    C. in meeting both of these needs equally
    D. in increased effort to define the motivational
       and maintenance needs of its employees

19. In accordance with the above article, which of the fol-   19.___
    lowing *CANNOT* be considered as an example of an employee
    maintenance need for railroad clerks?
    A. Providing more relief periods
    B. Providing fair salary increases at periodic intervals
    C. Increasing job responsibilities
    D. Increasing health insurance benefits

20. Most employees in an organization may be categorized as   20.___
    being interested in
    A. maintenance needs only   B. motivational needs only
    C. both motivational and maintenance needs
    D. money only, to the exclusion of all other needs

_____

KEY (CORRECT ANSWERS)

1.	A		11.	D
2.	A		12.	B
3.	D		13.	C
4.	C		14.	C
5.	B		15.	A
6.	C		16.	D
7.	B		17.	C
8.	A		18.	A
9.	D		19.	C
10.	B		20.	C

_____

TEST 2

1. The following are possible actions that a railroad clerk could take when a passenger tells him that he lost money in a malfunctioning token vending machine:
    I. Close the coin slot on the vending machine
    II. List the name and address of the passenger on the prescribed form
    III. Refund the lost amount of money to the passenger
    IV. Notify the station department control desk

    Which of the following choices lists *all* the correct actions stated above that the railroad clerk should take?
    A. I and II   B. I, II and III
    C. I, II and IV   D. II and IV

    1.___

2. Assume that 326 railroad porters will begin using a new type of disinfectant at certain stations as part of a test to determine the suitability of the disinfectant for authority use. If 1½ ounces of undiluted disinfectant must be added to 3 gallons of water to make a satisfactory solution of the disinfectant and each porter is expected to use approximately 5 gallons of disinfectant solution each week, the amount of undiluted disinfectant needed for *all* the porters for a 6-week test is
    A. 3890 ounces   B. 4890 ounces
    C. 4990 ounces   D. 5890 ounces

    2.___

3. Below are *four* possible actions which may or may not be taken in dealing with snow or sleet storms in accordance with standard operating procedures:
    I. Superintendents and station supervisors will communicate with the assistant general superintendent or his designated alternate for any special assignments.
    II. Assistant station supervisors who do not have a telephone at home will be required to communicate with their field office for assignment and if no assignment is given they will report for their next regularly assigned tour of duty.
    III. When a storm is of such severity that assistance from the bureau of track and structures is required, the supervisor on duty in the station department office will make such request to the ranking official of the bureau of track and structures.
    IV. On elevated stations where there are open ties, snow may be thrown between the running rails if extreme care is used to prevent tripping of trains.

    Which of the following choices lists *all* of the above procedures that are correct and *none* that is incorrect?
    A. I and III   B. II and III
    C. II and IV   D. III and IV

    3.___

4. If the total number of accidents to the public on authority property in May, 1992 was 529 and in May, 1993 was 585, the *percent increase* in accidents in May, 1993 as compared to May, 1992 is closest to

    A. 7%   B. 9%   C. 11%   D. 13%

4.___

5. You are instructing a newly appointed assistant station supervisor on the procedures for making a semi-annual inspection of a concession on authority property. You should tell him that if the concession has *NO* cooking facilities, he should check whether the concessionaire has on his premises a

    A. 2 lb. dry chemical fire extinguisher
    B. 5 lb. dry chemical fire extinguisher
    C. 2½ gallon water-type pressurized fire extinguisher
    D. 10 lb. capacity carbon dioxide fire extinguisher

5.___

6. The repair of malfunctioning public address speakers in the vicinity of token booths is the responsibility of the

    A. telephone subdivision   B. station department
    C. rapid transit operations department
    D. signal division

6.___

7. A wooden edging, level with the floor of a concrete platform and running its entire length, which is used to reduce the gap between the platform and a train is called a

    A. rubbing board   B. coping
    C. pantograph   D. slap rail

7.___

8. A railroad clerk, paid $11.48 an hour, works a 7:00 A.M. to 3:00 P.M. tour of duty Monday through Friday. What is his gross pay for a particular week if he is ordered to instruct a newly-appointed railroad clerk in the performance of his duties in his booth each day of that week during his tour?

    A. $482.16   B. $516.60   C. $533.82   D. $539.56

8.___

9. Assume that your superintendent has asked you to research a problem and to provide him with all the information necessary for him to arrive at a solution. In assembling this information you should be *especially* careful to give him *only* information which

    A. has been collected objectively
    B. will be consistent with previous information on this problem
    C. supports the present thinking of your superintendent
    D. in your judgment will provide the best solution to the problem

9.___

10. The following are possible supervisory practices which   10.___
a station supervisor might employ to create a healthy
climate for work, morale, and discipline among his sub-
ordinates:
   I. Tell subordinates that he will not answer questions
      which are covered by the book of rules
  II. Encourage subordinates to ask questions when in
      doubt about station department policies
 III. Praise subordinates in public, but reprimand them
      in private
  IV. Warn subordinates that they should feel guilty about
      making a mistake
   V. When a mistake is made, immediately institute disci-
      plinary action regardless of the causes
  VI. If a subordinate makes a significant mistake, use the
      opportunity to teach him the correct procedure

Which one of the following choices contains *only* those of
the above supervisory practices which are helpful for a
station supervisor to follow in creating a healthy climate
for work, morale, and discipline?
  A. I, II, and IV   B. I, IV, and V
  C. II, III, and VI   D. III, IV, and V

11. When formulating the annual operating budget in the   11.___
station department, it is necessary to determine the
number of man-days required to cover the various work
programs. If the railroad porter's work program calls
for 2,354 daily tours, 2,163 Saturday tours, and 1,980
Sunday tours (including holidays), then the number of
man-days which are normally required to cover this one-
year work program without taking into account vacation
coverage is, *most nearly*,
  A. 730,000   B. 780,000   C. 830,000   D. 880,000

12. Assume that you are in charge of a field office. At the   12.___
beginning of your tour on a particular day you are faced
with the following *four* almost simultaneous situations:
   I. One of your railroad clerks has telephoned your
      assistant station supervisor and has asked that you
      return her call as soon as possible because she has
      a question about her daily fare report.
  II. One of your railroad porters at an elevated station
      has telephoned you to report that a small section
      of one of the concrete platforms has broken off and
      fallen to the street.
 III. A clerk from the chief of operation's office has
      telephoned you and has requested you to complete
      and submit to them a special material utilization
      report immediately, since it is urgently needed
      at their office.
  IV. One of your assistant station supervisors gives you
      a written message regarding important information
      that you must use in the preparation of a statistical
      report covering emergency actions taken during the
      preceding month.

Which one of the above four situations should you take care of *FIRST?*
    A. I   B. II   C. III   D. IV

13. A railroad clerk complains to you that a certain newly   13.___
    appointed assistant station supervisor under your super-
    vision has been making rude and insulting comments to
    her about her work. The following are offered as pos-
    sible actions that you could consider taking in this
    matter:
      I. Interview the railroad clerk personally and obtain
         as many details of the alleged incidents as possible
     II. Ask the railroad clerk to be patient with the as-
         sistant station supervisor as he is still nervous
         about his new duties
    III. Tell the railroad clerk to keep a daily log of her
         encounters with this assistant station supervisor
         and make a report to you in one week
     IV. Summon the assistant station supervisor and ask him
         for an explanation
      V. Summon the railroad clerk and explain that this is
         not your concern but more properly a matter for her
         union representative

    Which of the following choices lists the *BEST* of the
    above actions to be taken in handling this matter?
      A. I and II   B. I and IV   C. II and III D. IV and V

14. You have been assigned to evaluate three different new   14.___
    cleansing powders for tile surfaces and to recommend
    the use of one of them for the station department. In
    your investigation you have determined that all of the
    cleansers can do equally satisfactory jobs. Therefore,
    your recommendation of the cleanser to use should be
    based *PRIMARILY* on which one costs *least* per
      A. pound
      B. square foot of tile cleaned
      C. gallon of water used
      D. package

15. A station supervisor leaves written instructions in con-   15.___
    nection with a work matter for one of his assistant sta-
    tion supervisors, and, in these instructions, he clearly
    delegates authority to the latter to supervise the job.

    In this situation, it would be *BEST* if the assistant
    station supervisor
      A. uses his delegated authority to make any changes
         in the scope of the job and its related activities
         that he feels are necessary
      B. notifies the station supervisor each time he uses
         his delegated authority on the job
      C. goes to the station supervisor frequently to check
         out details of the job as it progresses
      D. goes to the station supervisor only if there are
         unusual problems

16. The assistant station supervisor in charge of a collec-   16.___
    tion train must make sure that the collection train, and,
    in particular, the car in which the revenue is carried,
    is *NEVER* left without *at least*

    A. one armed guard   B. two armed guards
    C. three armed guards   D. four armed guards

17. When a train derailment or other major emergency oc-   17.___
    curs, the *PRIMARY* source for information to the news
    media about details of the incident should be the

    A. director of public information and community re-
       lations
    B. executive officer, operations and maintenance
    C. emergency press center
    D. station department office

18. Making supervisory decisions should be based on sound,   18.___
    problem-solving principles. Following are five prin-
    ciples which you might consider in trying to solve
    difficult problems:

    I. Make sure you understand the problems you are
       expected to solve
    II. Make sure you have some idea of possible solutions
        before you start working on the problems
    III. Review the results of past decisions on similar
         problems to provide helpful precedents
    IV. Consider the possible solutions to the problems
        without taking into account their consequences
    V. Call on your associates for help, especially those
       with experience in the areas involved

    Which of the following choices lists *all* of the above
    principles which are correct and *none* that is incorrect?

    A. I, III, and V   B. I, II, and III
    C. II, IV, and V   D. III, IV, and V

19. A "no clearance area" in the subway is indicated by a   19.___
    sign that has diagonal stripes that are colored *alter-
    nately*

    A. red and white   B. red and black
    C. black and white   D. black and yellow

20. The operation and maintenance of station department   20.___
    facilities is a continuing process. A station super-
    visor should seek ways to improve the efficiency of
    those operations which he supervises by such means
    as changing established methods and procedures that
    appear wasteful and inefficient.

    The following are possible courses of action which
    could be taken when changing established methods and
    procedures:

     I. Make changes only when your subordinates agree to them
    II. Make changes quickly and quietly in order to avoid dissent
  III. Secure expert guidance before instituting unfamiliar procedures
   IV. Standardize operations which are performed on a continuing basis
    V. Discuss changes with your superintendent before putting them into practice

Which of the following choices lists *only* those actions stated above which are useful when changing established methods or procedures?
A. I, II, and III
B. I, II, III, and V
C. II, III, and IV
D. III, IV, and V

21. A location in the subway having a blue light should normally have which of the following types of equipment? An emergency alarm box
    A. *only*
    B. *and* a telephone only
    C. *and* a fire extinguisher only
    D. a telephone and a fire extinguisher

21.___

22. The train whistle or horn signal which is meant to be an alarm to persons on a station platform consists of
    A. one long blast
    B. two long blasts
    C. two short blasts
    D. a succession of short blasts

22.___

23. When removing bags of tokens from the reserve supply, railroad clerks are directed to place on sale the bag with the
    A. least number of tokens
    B. most number of tokens
    C. most recent date
    D. oldest date

23.___

24. A railroad clerk, paid $10.80 an hour, works a 7:00 A.M. to 3:00 P.M. tour of duty Monday through Friday. What is his gross pay for a particular day on which he is required to attend a class on a new station department procedure for two hours after the completion of his tour of duty?
    A. $86.40
    B. $108.00
    C. $118.80
    D. $129.60

24.___

25. After using up all time credited to him, a railroad clerk who is eligible to receive 60% sick pay may receive this benefit if he is off sick for a minimum of
    A. 9 or more consecutive working days
    B. 14 or more consecutive working days
    C. 21 or more consecutive working days
    D. 25 or more consecutive working days

25.___

KEY (CORRECT ANSWERS)

1.	C		11.	C
2.	B		12.	B
3.	D		13.	B
4.	C		14.	B
5.	C		15.	D
6.	A		16.	B
7.	A		17.	C
8.	B		18.	A
9.	A		19.	A
10.	C		20.	D

21.	D
22.	D
23.	D
24.	C
25.	A

EXAMINATION SECTION
TEST 1

DIRECTIONS: Each question or incomplete statement is followed by several suggested answers or completions. Select the one that *BEST* answers the question or completes the statement. *PRINT THE LETTER OF THE CORRECT ANSWER IN THE SPACE AT THE RIGHT.*

Questions 1 - 7.

DIRECTIONS: Questions 1 to 7 are based on the portion of a COMBINED RAILROAD CLERKS DAILY FARE REPORT shown on the next page. Some of the computed entries in this report may not be mathematically correct. In answering the questions, you are to determine the accuracy of certain computed entries. You are to assume that all entries which are not computed on this report but which are copies or transferred from another source, such as OPENING readings and TOKENS RECEIVED entries, are correct. *NO OTHER ASSUMPTIONS ABOUT THE CORRECTNESS OF ENTRIES CAN BE MADE.*

1. For John Doe's tour of duty, the entries made on line 1.___
   "T" in the OPENING and CLOSING columns are 199780 and 202628, respectively. Select the statement below which *BEST* describes the accuracy of these totals.
   A. The total in the OPENING column is incorrect.
   B. The total in the CLOSING column is incorrect.
   C. Both totals are incorrect.
   D. Both totals are correct.

2. For John Doe's tour of duty, the entries made in the 2.___
   DIFFERENCE column associated with the OPENING and CLOSING turnstile readings are shown as 1187, 162, 1546, and 63. Select the statement below which *BEST* describes the accuracy of these differences.
   A. 1187 is incorrect while 162, 1546 and 63 are correct.
   B. 1187 and 63 are incorrect while 1546 and 162 are correct.
   C. 63 is incorrect while 1187, 162 and 1546 are correct.
   D. 1187 and 1546 are incorrect while 162 and 63 are correct.

3. For John Doe's tour of duty, select the statement below 3.___
   which *BEST* describes the accuracy of the amount $896.80 which he computed for NET FARES AT TOKEN VALUE.
   A. It is correct.
   B. It should be $10.00 higher.
   C. It should be $100.00 higher.
   D. It should be $100.00 lower.

4. For John Doe's tour of duty, select the statement below 4.___
   which *BEST* describes the accuracy of the amount 5600 which he computed for TOTAL TOKEN RESERVE.
   A. It is correct.   B. It should be 6500 higher.
   C. It should be 500 higher.   D. It should be 3500 lower.

COMBINED RAILROAD CLERKS DAILY FARE REPORT

BEGINNING AT ☐ 10PM ☒ 11PM ☐ 12 M ☐ Other ____ *MONDAY* DAY _1/619_ ENDING AT ☐ 10PM ☒ 11PM ☐ 12 M ☐ Other ____ *TUES.* DAY

Column No. ☐ 1   Column No. ☐ 2

	Column 1	Column 2
NAME (Print)	JOHN DOE	JOE SMITH
Time from	11PM to 7AM	7AM to 3PM
Pass #	17893W	18495X

Column No. 1 — JOHN DOE

	Opening Reading at 10PM	Closing Reading at 6AM	Difference	Audit (Leave Blank)
1	85 123	86 210	1 187	
2	63 264	63 426	162	
3	20 126	21 672	1 546	
4	31 267	31 320	63	
5				
6				
7				
8				
9				
10				
T	199 780	202 628	2 848	

Add Unregistered Fares (explain in remarks)

TOTAL FARES — 2848

Deduct: Slugs, mutilated foreign tokens registered in turnstiles — -
Test Rings-Turnstile # — -

NET FARES — 2848

1 NET FARES AT TOKEN VALUE	$8?6	80
Token Reserve at Start	6100	
Add Tokens Received	3000	
Deduct Tokens Transferred Out	3500	
TOTAL TOKEN RESERVE	5600	
Deduct Token Reserve at End	5600	
2 Value of Reserve Tokens Sold	- -	
TOTAL ADD (LINES 1-2)	$896	80
Add Remittance for Prior Shortage		
Deduct Deduction for Prior Overage	11	15
NET AMOUNT DUE	$907	15

Column No. 2 — JOE SMITH

	Opening Reading at 6AM	Closing Reading at 2PM	Difference	Audit (Leave Blank)
1	86 210	87 489	1 279	
2	63 422	65 897	2 475	
3	21 672	22 908	1 236	
4	31 320	31 962	642	
5				
6				
7				
8				
9				
10				
T	202 624	207 256	5 632	

Add Unregistered Fares (explain in remarks) — 11

TOTAL FARES — 5632

Deduct: Slugs, mutilated foreign tokens registered in turnstiles — 23
Test Rings-Turnstile # — 6

NET FARES — 5603

1 NET FARES AT TOKEN VALUE	$1961	05
Token Reserve at Start	5600	
Add Tokens Received	1400	
Deduct Tokens Transferred Out	2100	
TOTAL TOKEN RESERVE	4900	
Deduct Token Reserve at End	3242	
2 Value of Reserve Tokens Sold	1758	$ 615 30
TOTAL ADD (LINES 1-2)		$2576 35
Add Remittance for Prior Shortage		
Deduct Deduction for Prior Overage		
NET AMOUNT DUE		$2576 35

Rec'd. (Leave Blank)   Rec'd. (Leave Blank)

5. For Joe Smith's tour of duty, select the statement below   5.___
which *BEST* describes the accuracy of the CLOSING total
of 207256 computed by him.
    A. It is correct.   B. It is too high by 100.
    C. It is too low by 1000.   D. It is too low by 10000.

6. For Joe Smith's tour of duty, select the statement below   6.___
which *BEST* describes the accuracy of the NET FARES entry
of 5603.
    A. It is correct.   B. It is too low by 11.
    C. It is too low by 29.   D. It is too low by 36.

7. For Joe Smith's tour of duty, select the statement below   7.___
which *BEST* describes the accuracy of the amount $615.30
which he computed for the VALUE OF RESERVE TOKENS SOLD.
    A. It is correct.   B. It is too low by $1.00.
    C. It is too high by $25.00.   D. It is too high by $35.00.

Questions 8 - 14.

DIRECTIONS: Questions 8 to 14 are based on the portion of a COM-
BINED RAILROAD CLERKS DAILY FARE REPORT shown on the
next page. Some of the computed entries in this report may not be mathematically correct. In answering
the questions, you are to determine the accuracy of
certain computed entries. You are to assume that all
entries which are not computed on this report but which
are copies or transferred from another source, such as
OPENING readings and TOKENS RECEIVED entries, are correct. *NO OTHER ASSUMPTIONS ABOUT THE CORRECTNESS OF
ENTRIES CAN BE MADE.*

8. For Mary Spring's tour of duty, the entries made in the   8.___
DIFFERENCE column associated with the OPENING and CLOSING
turnstile readings are shown as 656, 1045, 1494, and 797.
Select the statement below which *BEST* describes the accuracy of these differences computed by her.
    A. 1045 is incorrect while 656, 1494 and 797 are correct.
    B. 1494 is incorrect while 656, 1045 and 797 are correct.
    C. 797 is incorrect while 656, 1045 and 1494 are correct.
    D. 656, 1045, 1494 and 797 are all correct.

9. For Mary Spring's tour of duty, select the statement which 9.___
BEST describes the accuracy of the OPENING total of 189466.
    A. It is correct.   B. It is too low by 10.
    C. It is too low by 100.   D. It is too high by 100.

10. For Mary Spring's tour of duty, select the statement   10.___
which *BEST* describes the accuracy of the NET FARES entry
of 3999.
    A. It is correct.   B. It is too low by 28.
    C. It is too high by 42.   D. It is too high by 14.

11. For Mary Spring's tour of duty, select the statement be-   11.___
low which *BEST* describes the accuracy of the amount 5800
which she computed for TOTAL TOKEN RESERVE.
    A. It is correct.   B. It is too low by 3400.
    C. It is too low by 1000.   D. It is too high by 2400.

COMBINED RAILROAD CLERKS DAILY FARE REPORT

BEGINNING AT ☒ 10 PM / 11 PM / 12 M / Other _WEDNES.DAY 1/2219___ ENDING AT ☒ 10 PM / 11 PM / 12 M / Other _THURS.DAY_

Column No.	1		Column No.	2

NAME (Print) *MARY SPRING*			NAME (Print) *HELEN FALL*		
Time from *11PM* to *7AM*		Pass # 30456Y	Time from *7AM* to *3PM*		Pass # 79346T

	Opening Reading at *10PM*	Closing Reading at *6AM*	Differ-ence	Audit (Leave Blank)	Opening Reading at *6AM*	Closing Reading at *2PM*	Differ-ence	Audit (Leave Blank)
1	34 767	35 423	656		35 423	36 411	988	
2	56 689	57 734	1 045		57 734	58 856	1 122	
3	76 474	77 968	1 494		77 968	78 649	681	
4	21 546	22 343	797		22 343	22 987	644	
5								
6								
7								
8								
9								
10								
T	189 466	193 468	3 992		193 368	196 803	3 435	
Add Unregistered Fares (explain in remarks)			14				17	
TOTAL FARES			3978				3452	
Deduct Slugs, mutilated foreign tokens registered in turnstiles			17				14	
Test Rings-- Turnstile #			4				3	
NET FARES			3999				3435	

1 NET FARES AT TOKEN VALUE	$1399 65	1 NET FARES AT TOKEN VALUE	$1202 25
Token Reserve at Start	6300	Token Reserve at Start	5800
Add Tokens Received	1200	Add Tokens Received	1400
Deduct Tokens Transferred Out	1700	Deduct Tokens Transferred Out	2700
TOTAL TOKEN RESERVE	5800	TOTAL TOKEN RESERVE	4500
Deduct Token Reserve at End	5800	Deduct Token Reserve at End	1943
2 Value of Reserve Tokens Sold	- - / - - -	2 Value of Reserve Tokens Sold	2657 / $ 929 95
TOTAL ADD (LINES 1-2)	$1399 65	TOTAL ADD (LINES 1-2)	$2132 20
Add Remittance for Prior Shortage		Add Remittance for Prior Shortage	4 30
Deduct Deduction for Prior Overage		Deduct Deduction for Prior Overage	
NET AMOUNT DUE	$1399 65	NET AMOUNT DUE	$2136 50

Rec'd. (Leave Blank)   Rec'd. (Leave Blank)

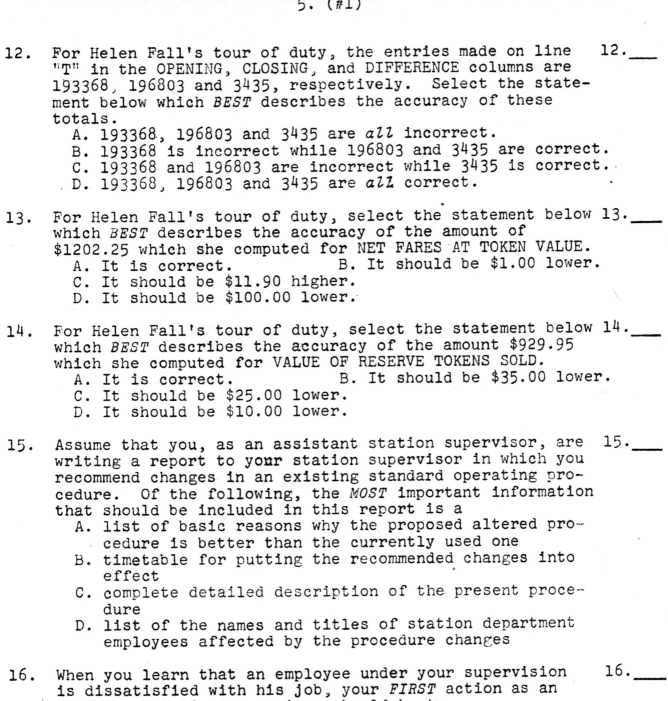

12. For Helen Fall's tour of duty, the entries made on line   12.___
    "T" in the OPENING, CLOSING, and DIFFERENCE columns are
    193368, 196803 and 3435, respectively. Select the state-
    ment below which *BEST* describes the accuracy of these
    totals.
    A. 193368, 196803 and 3435 are *all* incorrect.
    B. 193368 is incorrect while 196803 and 3435 are correct.
    C. 193368 and 196803 are incorrect while 3435 is correct.
    D. 193368, 196803 and 3435 are *all* correct.

13. For Helen Fall's tour of duty, select the statement below 13.___
    which *BEST* describes the accuracy of the amount of
    $1202.25 which she computed for NET FARES AT TOKEN VALUE.
    A. It is correct.   B. It should be $1.00 lower.
    C. It should be $11.90 higher.
    D. It should be $100.00 lower.

14. For Helen Fall's tour of duty, select the statement below 14.___
    which *BEST* describes the accuracy of the amount $929.95
    which she computed for VALUE OF RESERVE TOKENS SOLD.
    A. It is correct.   B. It should be $35.00 lower.
    C. It should be $25.00 lower.
    D. It should be $10.00 lower.

15. Assume that you, as an assistant station supervisor, are   15.___
    writing a report to your station supervisor in which you
    recommend changes in an existing standard operating pro-
    cedure. Of the following, the *MOST* important information
    that should be included in this report is a
    A. list of basic reasons why the proposed altered pro-
       cedure is better than the currently used one
    B. timetable for putting the recommended changes into
       effect
    C. complete detailed description of the present proce-
       dure
    D. list of the names and titles of station department
       employees affected by the procedure changes

16. When you learn that an employee under your supervision   16.___
    is dissatisfied with his job, your *FIRST* action as an
    assistant station supervisor should be to
    A. refer the matter to your station supervisor
    B. try to find out the reason for his dissatisfaction
    C. warn the employee not to spread his complaints to
       others
    D. tell the employee that since others are not dis
       satisfied he should not be

Questions 17 - 21.

DIRECTIONS: Questions 17 to 21 require computing basic schedule
              working time for certain specified tasks for porters.
              You are to use the AVERAGE WORKING TIME FOR ONE PORTER,
              which is shown at the top of the next page in the table,
              in computing the answers to these questions.

AVERAGE WORKING TIME FOR ONE PORTER

Task	Time
Sweeping Stairways	8 minutes per stairway
Scrapping Floor Areas	15,000 square feet per hour
Sweeping Floor Areas	5,500 square feet per hour
Cleaning Tile (7 to 9 ft. high)	50 linear feet per hour
Cleaning Tile (10 to 12 ft. high)	40 linear feet per hour
Cleaning Columns	6 per hour

17. A station has tile walls that are 7-1/2 ft. high. The
    TOTAL computed time for cleaning 3,735 linear feet of
    the tile in this station once a month is, *most nearly*,
    A. 7.5 hours B. 9.3 hours C. 74.7 hours D. 93.4 hours   17.___

18. The TOTAL computed time for cleaning 126 columns in a
    station once a month over a period of one year is   18.___
    A. 21 hours   B. 61 hours   C. 252 hours D. 1512 hours

19. The TOTAL weekly computed time for scrapping the floor
    area of a station having a northbound platform area of   19.___
    14,640 square feet and a southbound platform area of
    14,260 square feet three times a week is *closest to*
    A. 5 hours and 47 minutes   B. 5 hours and 17 minutes
    C. 3 hours and 10 minutes   D. 1 hour and 55 minutes

20. The TOTAL weekly computed time for sweeping seven stair-   20.___
    ways twice a week at a station is
    A. 56 min.   B. 1 hour and 52 minutes
    C. 2 hours and 2 minutes   D. 2 hours and 12 minutes

21. The TOTAL weekly computed time for sweeping both the   21.___
    northbound and southbound platforms of a station, where
    each has a floor area of 13,670 square feet, twice a
    week, is *closest to*
    A. 4.9 hours B. 8.8 hours C. 9.9 hours D. 19.9 hours

22. One of the railroad clerks in a booth sees a passenger,   22.___
    who appears to be intoxicated and unable to take care
    of himself, outside the booth stumbling towards a turn-
    stile. Following are four possible courses of action
    which this railroad clerk could take which might be cor-
    rect:
    I. Have the passenger placed in the charge of a transit
       patrolman
    II. Have the passenger placed in the charge of an assist-
       ant station supervisor
    III. Allow the passenger to pay his fare and enter through
       the turnstile if there is a transit patrolman present
    IV. Allow the passenger to pay his fare and enter through
       the turnstile, but don't allow him to go onto the
       platform without assistance

    Which of the following choices lists ALL of the above
    courses of action that are *correct* and lists *NONE* that is
    incorrect?
    A. I and II   B. I, II, and III
    C. I and III   D. II and IV

23. With the exception of those keys under the jurisdiction   23.___
    of the transportation department, the keys to the emer-
    gency rooms at the end of each rapid transit river tunnel
    are kept
       A. at designated booths at either end of the tunnels
       B. at the nearest field office
       C. by assistant station supervisors
       D. in special lockers outside these rooms

24. Part of a rule for assistant station supervisors states   24.___
    as follows:

    He will keep a running inventory showing the supplies
    received and the distribution made by date and by station.

    Of the following, the idea which is *CLOSEST* to the basic
    meaning of the above instruction is that assistant station
    supervisors must
       A. keep a continuous record of supplies received and
          distributed
       B. keep an accurate record of the cost of supplies re-
          ceived and distributed
       C. periodically update their summary inventories
       D. maintain a fast moving inventory

25. When a supervisor gives instructions to a subordinate   25.___
    employee about a specific task, the amount of detailed
    information that the supervisor should give him depends
    PRIMARILY on
       A. the difficulty of the job and how long the job will
          take
       B. the difficulty of the job and the amount of experi-
          ence the employee has
       C. how long the job will take and the amount of experi-
          ence the employee has
       D. how long the job will take and how much time the sub-
          ordinate has to listen

KEY (CORRECT ANSWERS)

1.	D	6.	B	11.	A	16.	B	21.	C
2.	B	7.	D	12.	C	17.	C	22.	A
3.	C	8.	D	13.	A	18.	C	23.	A
4.	A	9.	B	14.	B	19.	A	24.	A
5.	C	10.	D	15.	A	20.	B	25.	B

TEST 2

DIRECTIONS: Each question or incomplete statement is followed by several suggested answers or completions. Select the one that *BEST* answers the question or completes the statement. *PRINT THE LETTER OF THE CORRECT ANSWER IN THE SPACE AT THE RIGHT.*

1. When an employee has discovered a fire on transit author- 1.___
   ity property and has used a fire extinguisher to put out
   the fire, he should return the extinguisher to the exact
   location from which it was taken, *PRIMARILY* so that
   A. it will not be reported missing
   B. it will be ready for immediate reuse in case of
      another fire
   C. it is placed out of the way and will not be a tripping
      hazard
   D. no delay will occur in having it refilled

Questions 2 - 6.

DIRECTIONS: Questions 2 to 6 are based on the paragraphs shown below entitled, "Posting of Diversion of Service Notices."
Refer to these paragraphs when answering these questions.

POSTING OF DIVERSION OF SERVICE NOTICES

The following procedures concerning the receiving and posting of
service diversion notices will be strictly adhered to:

Assistant station supervisors who receive notices will sign a
receipt and return it to the Station Department office. It will be
their responsibility to ensure that all notices are posted at affected stations and a notation made in the transmittal logs. All
excess notices will be tied and a notation made thereon, indicating
the stations and the date notices were posted, and the name and
pass number of the assistant station supervisor posting same. The
word "Excess" is to be boldly written on bundled notices and the
bundle placed in a conspicuous location. When loose notices, without any notations, are discovered in any field office, assistant
station supervisor's office or other Station Department locations,
the matter is to be thoroughly investigated to make sure proper
distribution has been completed. All stations where a diversion
of service exists must be contacted daily by the assistant station
supervisor covering that group and hour to ensure that a sufficient
number of notices are posted and employees are aware of the situation. In any of the above circumstances, notation is to be made
in the supervisory log. Station supervisors will be responsible
for making certain all affected stations in their respective groups
have notices posted and for making spot checks each day diversions
are in effect.

2. An assistant station supervisor who has signed a receipt 2.___
   upon receiving service diversion notices must return the
   A. notice to the Station Department office
   B. receipt to the Station Department office
   C. receipt and the transmittal log to the affected
      stations
   D. transmittal log after making a notation in it

3. Of the following, the information which is *NOT* required   3.___
   to be written on a bundle of excess notices is the
   - A. names of the stations where the notices were posted
   - B. time of day when the notices were posted
   - C. date when the notices were posted
   - D. name and pass number of the assistant station super-
     visor posting the notices

4. If loose notices without notations on them are found, the   4.___
   situation should be investigated to make sure that the
   - A. notices are properly returned to the Station Department
   - B. assistant station supervisor responsible for the
     error is found
   - C. notices are correct for the diversion involved
   - D. notices have been distributed properly

5. To insure that employees are aware of a diversion in ser-   5.___
   vice, an assistant station supervisor covering the group
   and hour when a diversion exists must contact the involved
   stations
   - A. immediately after the diversion
   - B. on an hourly basis
   - C. on a daily basis
   - D. as often as possible

6. To make certain affected stations have notices posted   6.___
   when diversions occur, *spot checks* should be made by
   - A. station supervisors daily
   - B. station supervisors when necessary
   - C. assistant station supervisors daily
   - D. assistant station supervisors when necessary

7. An employee who has been absent due to illness must submit 7.___
   a sick leave application *within*
   - A. two days after his return to work
   - B. three days after his return to work
   - C. five days after his return to work
   - D. one week after his return to work

8. Except at heavily traveled areas, the rear section of all   8.___
   trains will be closed off and isolated between the hours
   of
   - A. 7 p.m. and 5 p.m. daily   B. 8 p.m. and 4 a.m. daily
   - C. 9 p.m. and 6 a.m. daily   D. 10 p.m. and 5 a.m. daily

9. A passenger notices that you, an assistant station super-   9.___
   visor, have come out of a booth and he angrily complains
   to you about poor subway conditions.

   Of the following, the *BEST* procedure for you to follow
   in this case is to
   - A. listen to him courteously and avoid, if possible,
     making any argumentative statements
   - B. tell the passenger to complain to the mayor's office
   - C. tell the passenger that nothing can be done about the
     situation because of current budgetary problems
   - D. indicate to the passenger that you agree with him

10. If a supervisor finds it necessary for the first time to criticize a subordinate for poor work performance, it is *MOST* important that he should
    A. make sure that the subordinate is in a good mood before criticizing him
    B. make sure others are present in order to set an example for them also
    C. be specific in his criticism to the subordinate
    D. criticize the subordinate harshly to make sure his performance improves

11. According to the station department manual of instructions, the major duties performed by a porter at a station are defined as those duties that
    A. are more important than others
    B. involve greater physical effort to perform
    C. are performed daily
    D. are performed on certain days of the week

12. The transit authority rules state that an employee must undergo a medical examination by the transit authority medical staff before being permitted to return to work if he has been absent on sick leave *more than*
    A. 14 consecutive calendar days
    B. 21 consecutive calendar days
    C. 28 consecutive calendar days
    D. 35 consecutive calendar days

Questions 13 - 18.

DIRECTIONS: Questions 13 to 18 are based on the chart of HOURLY TURNSTILE READINGS shown below. Refer to this chart when answering these questions.

HOURLY TURNSTILE READINGS

Turnstile No.	2 P.M.	3 P.M.	4 P.M.	5 P.M.	6 P.M.
1	79062	81134	81968	82450	83639
2	38829	39663	40243	42598	44333
3	14376	14693	14898	14987	15036
4	55444	55582	55647	55839	55989

13. The turnstile which registered the *LARGEST* number of fares between 3 P.M. and 5 P.M. is
    A. No. 1   B. No. 2   C. No. 3   D. No. 4

14. The turnstile which registered the *LOWEST* number of fares between 2 P.M. and 3 P.M. is
    A. No. 1   B. No. 2   C. No. 3   D. No. 4

15. The *total number* of passengers using Turnstile No. 2 from 2 P.M. to 6 P.M. is
    A. 5504   B. 5505   C. 5515   D. 5604

16. The *total number* of passengers using all four turnstiles from 3 P.M. to 4 P.M. is
    A. 1574   B. 1674   C. 1684   D. 1784

17. Turnstile No. 1 registered the *LOWEST* number of passen-   17.___
    gers between
    A. 2 P.M. and 3 P.M.   B. 3 P.M. and 4 P.M.
    C. 4 P.M. and 5 P.M.   D. 5 P.M. and 6 P.M.

18. Turnstile No. 3 registered the *HIGHEST* number of passen-   18.___
    gers between
    A. 2 P.M. and 3 P.M.   B. 3 P.M. and 4 P.M.
    C. 4 P.M. and 5 P.M.   D. 5 P.M. and 6 P.M.

19. According to the rules and regulations, a railroad clerk   19.___
    who calls in sick must do so *at least*
    A. 1/2 hour before the start of his tour of duty
    B. 2 hour before the start of his tour of duty
    C. 2 hours before the start of his tour of duty
    D. 3 hours before the start of his tour of duty

20. The location of an emergency alarm box for removing   20.___
    third rail power is indicated by
    A. a red light   B. three amber lights
    C. a lunar white light   D. a blue light

21. The information contained in station department bulletin   21.___
    orders covers *PRIMARILY*
    A. revisions in the station department manual of in-
       structions
    B. matters of ordinary routine for all employees
    C. instructions for non-supervisory employees
    D. matters of an operational nature which are usually
       permanent

22. The train horn signal consisting of a series of long-   22.___
    short-long-short blasts means that the train
    A. crew needs assistance   B. needs a road car inspector
    C. is passing caution lights or flags and is warning a
       flagman of its approach
    D. has run past or stopped short of the station platform

23. Of the following, the *BEST* course of action for an as-   23.___
    sistant station supervisor to follow when he observes a
    porter for the first time scrapping a platform in an un-
    satisfactory way is to
    A. reprimand the porter and tell him to do better the
       next time
    B. make several more checks on the porter to determine
       whether he does his other tasks satisfactorily
    C. discuss the situation with his station supervisor
    D. demonstrate to the porter the proper way of doing
       the work and then observe him doing it

24. In case an assistant station supervisor sees smoke in   24.___
    the subway, he should *immediately* call the
    A. fire department   B. desk trainmaster
    C. transit police   D. maintenance of way department

25. If a porter observes an unauthorized vendor selling his   25.___
    goods in a station, the porter should *immediately* report
    this to

A. the police
B. his assistant station supervisor
C. the office of the assistant general superintendent,
   stations
D. the transit police

———

KEY (CORRECT ANSWERS)

1.	D		11.	D	
2.	B		12.	B	
3.	B		13.	B	
4.	D		14.	D	
5.	C		15.	A	
6.	A		16.	C	
7.	B		17.	C	
8.	B		18.	A	
9.	A		19.	B	
10.	C		20.	D	

21.	D
22.	A
23.	D
24.	B
25.	D

———

TEST 3

DIRECTIONS: Each question or incomplete statement is followed by several suggested answers or completions. Select the one that *BEST* answers the question or completes the statement. *PRINT THE LETTER OF THE CORRECT ANSWER IN THE SPACE AT THE RIGHT.*

1. Each employee who receives lost property will be held responsible for it
   A. and will be able to claim it as his own after three months
   B. unless he can produce a receipt for it from another employee
   C. until it is claimed by its owner
   D. until the time it reaches the Lost Property Office

   1.___

2. The *total number* of zones that the station department operates is
   A. 4   B. 6   C. 8   D. 10

   2.___

3. At 11:00 A.M., on a Tuesday, a porter reports to his assistant station supervisor that a heavy piece of equipment fell on him and injured his foot. Unless the employee needs immediate hospital attention, the *PROPER* course of action for the assistant station supervisor to take is to
   A. have the porter make out an accident report and send him to a transit authority clinic
   B. fill out an accident report and tell the porter to continue his normal duties
   C. tell the porter to sign out and see his family doctor if necessary
   D. tell the porter to go back to his job and wait for a replacement before going home

   3.___

4. In an emergency, when it is necessary to remove power from the third rail and there is no emergency alarm box available, power may be removed by telephoning the
   A. station department office, control desk
   B. power distribution division
   C. nearest train dispatcher
   D. desk trainmaster of the division involved

   4.___

5. When a low turnstile at a station become inoperative, the railroad clerk on duty must *immediately* notify
   A. his assistant station supervisor
   B. the station department office, control desk
   C. the turnstile subdivision, maintenance of way department
   D. the appropriate field office

   5.___

6. The train horn signal consisting of two long blasts means that the train
   A. crew needs assistance
   B. needs a signal maintainer
   C. is passing caution lights or flags and is warning a flagman of its approach
   D. is passing through the station without stopping

   6.___

7. A person has been injured by tripping and falling down   7.___
the stairs in a station and has been given assistance by
a railroad clerk. The railroad clerk finds it necessary
to turn over the injured person to the care of another
transit authority employee.

For the purpose of filling out the necessary reports,
both employees must exchange
   A. names and pass numbers only
   B. names, titles, and pass numbers
   C. names and titles only
   D. names, titles, and assigned work locations

8. A booth in a station that is manned continuously and   8.___
where the railroad clerk is in general charge of the
station is classified as a(n)
   A. station head booth   B. area control booth
   C. transfer booth   D. 24-hour booth

9. The transfer of change funds from one station booth to   9.___
another
   A. is never permitted
   B. is permitted without any special authorization
   C. can be made between part-time booths and control
      booths
   D. is permitted in emergencies if authorized by a
      railroad clerk in general charge of a station

Questions 10 - 14.

DIRECTIONS: Questions 10 to 14 are based on the paragraphs shown
               below covering the supply duties of assistant station
               supervisors. Refer to these paragraphs when answering
               these questions.

SUPPLY DUTIES OF ASSISTANT STATION SUPERVISORS

The assistant station supervisors on the 8 a.m. to 4 p.m. tour
will be responsible for the ordering of porter cleaning supplies and
will inventory individual stations under their jurisdiction in order
to maintain the necessary supplies to insure proper sanitary standards. They will be responsible not only for the ordering of such
supplies but will see to it that ordered supplies are distributed as
required in accordance with order supply sheets. Assistant station
supervisors on the 4 p.m. to 12 midnight and 12 midnight to 8 a.m.
shift will cooperate with the a.m. station supervisor to properly
control supplies.

The 4 p.m. to 12 midnight assistant station supervisors will be
responsible for the ordering and control of all stationery supplies
used by railroad clerks in the performance of their duties. They
will also see that supplies are kept in a neat and orderly manner.
The assistant station supervisors in charge of "Supply Storerooms"
will see to it that material so ordered will be given to the porters
for delivery to the respective booths. Cooperation of all supervision applies in this instance.

The 12 midnight to 8 a.m. assistant station supervisors will be responsible for the storing of materials delivered by special work train (sawdust, etc.). They will also see that all revenue bags which are torn, dirty, etc., are picked up and sent to the field office for delivery to the bag room.

Any supplies needed other than those distributed on regular supply days will be requested by submitting a requisition to the supply control desk for emergency delivery.

10. The assistant station supervisors who are responsible   10.____
    for ordering all stationery supplies used by railroad
    clerks are the ones on the
       A. 8 a.m. to 4 p.m. tour
       B. 4 p.m. to 12 midnight tour
       C. 12 midnight to 8 a.m. tour
       D. 4 p.m. to 2 p.m. tour

11. Storing of materials delivered by special work trains   11.____
    is the responsibility of assistant station supervisors
    on the
       A. 8 a.m. to 4 p.m. tour
       B. 4 p.m. to 12 midnight tour
       C. 12 midnight to 8 a.m. tour
       D. 4 p.m. to 2 p.m. tour

12. Torn revenue bags should be picked up and sent *FIRST* to   12.____
       A. the bag room   B. the supply control desk
       C. a supply storeroom   D. the field office

13. To obtain an emergency delivery of supplies on a day   13.____
    other than a regular supply day, a requisition should
    be submitted to the
       A. appropriate zone office   B. appropriate field office
       C. supply control desk   D. station supervisor

14. The assistant station supervisor responsible for order-   14.____
    ing porter cleaning supplies will inventory individual
    stations *PRIMARILY* for the end purpose of
       A. insuring proper sanitary standards
       B. maintaining necessary supplies
       C. keeping track of supplies
       D. distributing supplies fairly

15. A collecting agent may reveal a combination to a safe if   15.____
    he
       A. has a written order from the superintendent of stations
       B. is verbally instructed to do so by the station super-
          visor
       C. reports this action in writing to the station depart-
          ment assistant general superintendent
       D. has the written permission of the assistant station
          supervisor to whom he reports

16. The train starting signal at terminal stations and the   16.____
    train holding signal at gap stations consist of *three*
       A. blue lights   B. lunar white lights
       C. red lights   D. amber lights

17. According to the rules and regulations, assistant station   17.___
supervisors have certain duties and responsibilities.

Following are four duties and responsibilities of assist-
ant station supervisors which might be correct:
   I. They report to station supervisors and to other
      superior officers of the station department and the
      rapid transit operations department.
  II. They are in charge of designated groups of stations
      or other designated areas.
 III. They determine that current work schedules for em-
      ployees under their jurisdiction provide efficient
      and effective service.
  IV. They supervise the installation of turnstiles in
      stations.

Which of the following choices lists *ALL* of the above
duties and responsibilities that are *correct* and lists
NONE that is *incorrect?*
    A. I, II, and III   B. I, II, III, and IV
    C. II and III   D. II, III, and IV

18. After a robbery has taken place at a booth, the railroad   18.___
clerk involved must take certain immediate steps.

Following are four *immediate* steps that might be correct:
   I. Notify the police using the appropriate telephone
      extension
  II. Notify the station department office and the field
      office
 III. Check the booth accounts and ascertain the loss
  IV. Submit a complete written report of the occurrence

Which of the following choices lists *ALL* of the above
steps that are *correct* and lists *NO* step that is *incorrect?*
    A. I, II, III, and IV   B. I, II, and IV
    C. I, III, and IV   D. II, III, and IV

19. When giving instructions to a porter, you will *most*   19.___
likely avoid confusing him if
    A. your instructions are as detailed as possible
    B. your instructions are clear and concise
    C. you repeat your instructions to him several times
       using different words each time
    D. you give him the instructions as quickly as possible

20. A supervisor who is performing his job well should be   20.___
checking all operations under his jurisdiction.

Of the following, the *LEAST* important reason for doing
this is to make certain that
    A. he personally observes all operations as they are
       performed
    B. all the operations are still needed
    C. subordinates are performing their work efficiently
    D. operations are being performed as scheduled

21. The train that goes to Far Rockaway is the   21.___

      A. "A" train   B. "E" train
      C. "F" train   D. number "2" train

22. In order to travel by subway to Ditmars Boulevard and   22.___
    31 Street in Astoria, it is necessary to take the
      A. "RR" train   B. "EE" train
      C. number "7" train   D. "M" train

23. The number "1" train travels between   23.___
      A. Pelham Bay Park and Brooklyn Bridge at Worth Street
      B. Van Cortlandt Park and South Ferry
      C. Woodlawn and Utica Avenue
      D. Dyre Avenue and Atlantic Avenue

24. When preparing a report about an unusual occurrence   24.___
    it is *LEAST* important to
      A. be accurate on the details
      B. make the report lengthy in description
      C. be clear in describing the incident
      D. leave out unimportant details

25. The transit authority sick leave "year" is defined as   25.___
    the period between
      A. January 1 and December 31   B. April 1 and March 31
      C. May 1 and April 30   D. July 1 and June 30

26. If an assistant station supervisor suspects that a porter 26.___
    is unfit for duty because of alcohol, he should
      A. ask the porter whether he can perform his work
      B. direct the porter to submit to a blood-alcohol
         examination
      C. suspend the porter and discipline him
      D. tell the porter to return to work when he sobers up

27. According to the station department manual of instruc-   27.___
    tions, a station department employee may exchange a tour
    of duty with another employee *provided* he has received
    specific permission from
      A. his immediate supervisor   B. his field office
      C. the station department office
      D. the assistant general superintendent, stations

28. A passenger tells a station department employee that he   28.___
    fell on a station platform and he wants to know how to
    file a claim against the transit authority.

    The *PROPER* procedure for the employee to follow is to
    tell the passenger
      A. that he cannot give him any information
      B. that he will file an accident report and a claim
         for damages for the passenger
      C. to leave his name and address and that a member of
         the transit authority managerial staff will contact
         him
      D. to contact the transit authority's law department
         at Jay Street

29. According to step 1 of the grievance procedure, a railroad clerk may present a grievance to his assistant station supervisor

29.___

    A. orally or through his union only
    B. orally or in writing personally only
    C. orally, in writing personally, or through his union
    D. in writing personally or through his union only

30. After an aggrieved railroad clerk has received a step 1 decision, he may appeal this decision within

30.___

    A. 48 hours   B. 3 days   C. 5 days   D. 1 week

KEY (CORRECT ANSWERS)

1.	B	11.	C	21.	A
2.	C	12.	D	22.	A
3.	A	13.	C	23.	B
4.	D	14.	A	24.	B
5.	B	15.	A	25.	C
6.	C	16.	D	26.	B
7.	B	17.	C	27.	C
8.	A	18.	D	28.	D
9.	C	19.	B	29.	C
10.	B	20.	A	30.	B

EXAMINATION SECTION
TEST 1

DIRECTIONS: Each question or incomplete statement is followed by several suggested answers or completions. Select the one that BEST answers the question or completes the statement.

1. Good supervision requires that the assistant station supervisor visit his assigned stations
   A. on a fixed schedule only
   B. as many times a day as possible
   C. only when trouble develops
   D. at random as well as regular intervals

2. At a subway station located in the financial district, an assistant station supervisor would normally expect the GREATEST concentration of passenger traffic to occur from
   A. 6:30 A.M. to 8:00 A.M.   B. 7:30 A.M. to 8:30 A.M.
   C. 4:00 P.M. to 5:30 P.M.   D. 5:30 P.M. to 7:30 P.M.

3. The LEAST important reason for the requirement that all accidents on the transit system must be promptly investigated is that such investigation helps to
   A. settle claims promptly
   B. fix responsibility
   C. set up a regular routine
   D. prevent similar accidents in the future

4. Two porters are to be assigned to a special cleaning job at a remote location. By placing the one with the better record in charge, the assistant supervisor will
   A. be showing good judgment
   B. know that the job will require no supervision on his part
   C. be following standard policy
   D. not be criticized if the job is poorly done

5. The BEST assurance an assistant station supervisor can have that a railroad clerk knows how to do his work is if the clerk
   A. makes few mistakes   B. is cooperative
   C. works quickly   D. asks no questions

6. An accident involving an employee occurred on a job to which you had assigned two men. In questioning them separately to fix responsibility, you should be MAINLY interested in obtaining information pertaining to
   A. the ability and experience of each
   B. how well the other understood your instructions
   C. the manner in which the other performs his work
   D. what each was doing at the time the accident occurred

7. For the sake of safety while working under conditions which
   involve an element of danger, safety rules have been compiled
   A. to eliminate accidents
   B. to minimize time lost
   C. for the guidance of employees
   D. for avoiding dangerous assignments

8. Six porters can clean a certain tile wall in 3 hours. If two
   of the porters left one hour after starting work, the job would
   require
   A. 3 1/2 hours   B. 4 hours   C. 5 hours   D. 9 hours

9. Of the following, the LEAST important element in good subway
   service is the
   A. size of the cars
   B. relative infrequency of breakdowns
   C. cleanliness of cars and stations
   D. courtesy of the employees

10. A report of an unusual occurrence is MOST likely to be accurate
    as to facts if written by the assistant station supervisor
    A. before discussing matters with anyone
    B. right after the occurrence
    C. after discussion with the station supervisor
    D. the following day after thinking things over

11. The assistant station supervisors on the 4 P.M. to midnight
    trick are responsible for the
    A. ordering and distribution of porter cleaning supplies
    B. storing of all special work train deliveries such as sawdust
    C. ordering and control of all stationery supplies used by
       railroad clerks
    D. for the collection of all torn and dirty revenue bags

12. If a porter reporting for duty falls and apparently sustains a
    broken leg, the assistant station supervisor should immediately
    telephone the
    A. nearest T.A. clinic   B. first aid room
    C. supervisor's office   D. transit police

Questions 13-19.

DIRECTIONS: Questions 13 through 19 are based on the description of
           a special event given below. Refer to this description
           in answering these questions.

   A special parade, on Thanksgiving Day, is to follow, for the first
time, a line of march paralleling a nearby 4-track rapid transit
line, and approximately 1 1/2 million spectators are anticipated.
The parade is expected to take 3 hours to pass any given point and
it will take 2 hours for any part of the parade to march from the
beginning to the end of the route, starting near the Cliff Street
express station at 10:00 A.M., marching north, and finishing near
the Bank Street express station. There are 5 local stops between
these points. No other rapid transit line is near the route of the
parade although several surface lines cross the line of march. One
terminal of the rapid transit line is about 30 minutes riding time

from Cliff station via express, the other terminal is about 35 minutes riding time from Bank station via express, and the scheduled riding time from Cliff station to Bank station is 10 minutes via local and 6 minutes via express.

13. From the description of the event it is clear that one who wished to go from the Bank Street station to the Cliff Street station would have to travel
    A. north   B. south   C. east   D. west

14. The employees of this rapid transit line should expect a large number of passengers to enter at Cliff Street station starting at about
    A. 11:00 A.M.   B. 12:00 Noon   C. 1:00 P.M.   D. 3:00 P.M.

15. The employees of this rapid transit line should expect a large number of passengers to enter at Bank Street station starting at about
    A. 12:00 Noon B. 1:00 P.M. C. 2:00 P.M.   D. 3:00 P.M.

16. The BEST place to make the count of passengers who come to watch the parade would be at
    A. the express stations   B. the local sations
    C. Bank Street   D. Cliff Street

17. If the local stops are uniformly spaced, the time it takes for any one part of the parade to march from one local station to the next is APPROXIMATELY
    A. 10 minutes B. 15 minutes   C. 20 minutes D. 30 minutes

18. The riding time between the terminals of this line, via express, is
    A. 35 minutes   B. 1 hour and 5 minutes
    C. 1 hour and 11 minutes D. 1 hour and 15 minutes

19. The BEST way to make the count of passengers who will probably use any particular station when the parade is over would be to
    A. assign personnel to all exits to count crowd leaving station
    B. count the number of tokens sold there to parade time
    C. take a turnstile count at that station until 12:00 P.M.
    D. estimate number of passengers exiting from trains stopping at that station

20. Ten car trains arrive on five minute intervals at a terminal station. Assuming that each car carries 120 passengers, the number of passengers exiting from the station in an hour is NEAREST to
    A. 8200   B. 12000   C. 14400   D. 16000

21. Of the following, the BEST way to have transit employees as a whole learn good safety habits is to
    A. penalize them with loss of pay for lost-time accidents
    B. let them learn through their own mistakes
    C. have them re-read the rules in their spare time
    D. offer prizes for the best safety records

22. To keep errors in station entrance computations to a minimum, turnstile meters
    A. are placed on each turnstile
    B. must be read at definite times
    C. require much maintenance
    D. have large and clear numbers

23. One of the duties of assistant station supervisors is to
    A. immediately report infractions of the rules which come to their attention
    B. check daily to see that railroad clerks and porters have ample supplies
    C. be responsible for any tools or equipment left by the turnstile section on any of the stations in his area
    D. make any changes in 'Station Department Instructions that are necessary

24. A porter complains to you that the porter he relieves does not complete his share of the work and that he has been informed that this is due to frequent and lengthy conversations with passengers. The LEAST likely conclusion would be that the porter complained of
    A. is well liked by the regular passengers at that station
    B. lives near the station
    C. is a responsible individual
    D. has had words with the porter turning him in

25. You have noticed that one of the porters at a station in your area is frequently in the tower at the end of the platform. He tells you that he is studying for the next railroad clerk promotion examination whenever he gets a chance. As assistant station supervisor you should
    A. overlook this situation since it is temporary and reasonable
    B. inform him that he is never permitted in the tower
    C. transfer the man to a station in the area without a tower
    D. insist that he discontinue this practice during working hours

26. A recently appointed porter is assigned to duty under your supervision. Of the following, the MOST important thing to do is
    A. make sure he knows all the rules and regulations in detail
    B. acquaint him with traffic conditions at his station
    C. familiarize him with the schedule of working conditions for station employees
    D. take him on a tour of the station to which he will be assigned pointing out his duties

27. A systematic layout of work and proper assignment of men to a special job, by an assistant supervisor, will NOT affect the
    A. amount of work to be done
    B. quality of the finished work
    C. time required to do the work
    D. kind of supervision needed in the performance of the work

28. An assistant station supervisor, telephoning from an agent's booth located on a subway platform, hears a train whistle signal that sounds to him like "short-long-short". If the signal is not repeated and the railroad clerk also is not sure of what he heard, the assistant station supervisor could logically conclude that he had heard part of a signal and that the motorman was actually signaling to alert
    A. people standing too close to the edge of the platform to move back
    B. station or police personnel that assistance is needed
    C. his conductor that the train will overrun or stop short of the station marker
    D. a car inspector to meet the train as something needs correction

29. A station having a total platform area of 22,575 sq. ft. is to be swept twice a week. If the average area that can be swept per hour is 5,250 sq. ft., the total time to be allotted for the twice-weekly sweeping is CLOSEST to
    A. 4 hours, 6 minutes   B. 4 hours, 18 minutes
    C. 8 hours, 36 minutes   D. 9 hours, 20 minutes

30. For three adjacent stations for the same period, the first requires twice as much sawdust as the second and the second twice as much as the third. If 14 bags of sawdust are to be properly distributed to these stations, the first station should receive
    A. 4 bags   B. 6 bags   C. 8 bags   D. 10 bags

———

KEY (CORRECT ANSWERS)

1.	D	11.	C		21.	D
2.	C	12.	D		22.	B
3.	C	13.	B		23.	A
4.	A	14.	C		24.	C
5.	A	15.	D		25.	D
6.	D	16.	A		26.	D
7.	C	17.	C		27.	A
8.	B	18.	C		28.	B
9.	A	19.	A		29.	C
10.	B	20.	C		30.	C

TEST 2

DIRECTIONS: Each question or incomplete statement is followed by several suggested answers or completions. Select the one that BEST answers the question or completes the statement.

1. The official published Rules and Regulations are LEAST useful in
   A. helping employees in the proper performance of their duties
   B. relieving supervisory employees of their responsibility
   C. providing a fair basis for any necessary disciplinary action
   D. encouraging safe practices

2. An employee of the transit system should give his name and badge number at the request of any passenger
   A. without argument after first trying to placate the passenger
   B. without delay or argument
   C. if a valid reason is given
   D. if the passenger insists strenuously

3. It is particularly important that assistant station supervisors be acquainted with the various rapid transit and surface lines in order to
   A. be able to move quickly to another point when necessary
   B. make the best disposition of passengers in case of blockade
   C. be able to make recommendations for better service
   D. generally answer passenger questions in this regard

4. Considerable time of supervision is required in investigating complaints by passengers against employees. The BEST overall solution to this problem is to
   A. have supervisors stress courtesy in public relations
   B. set up a central complaint bureau
   C. send a standard courteous answer and omit investigation
   D. investigate only the legitimate complaints

5. It would be POOR supervision on the part of an assistant station supervisor if he
   A. consulted an experienced railroad clerk on an unusual problem
   B. made it a policy to avoid criticizing a man while another was present
   C. overlooked minor infractions of the rules on occasions
   D. allowed several days to elapse before giving one of his men a deserved reprimand

Questions 6-11.

DIRECTIONS: Questions 6 through 11 are based on the tabulation of
Turnstile Readings shown below. Consult this tabulation
in answering these questions. Note that booth No. 74 is
open 24 hours a day, the clerk on the midnight tour reporting at 11:00 P.M.

TURNSTILE READINGS

BOOTH NO. 74 - WEST STREET STATION

Sunday - August 5, 19--

HOUR	TURNSTILE NUMBER				
	1	2	3	4	5
5 AM	72583	00602	08390	22924	98832
6 AM	72650	00631	08437	22983	98893
7 AM	72705	00648	08472	23031	98945
8 AM	72747	00659	08501	23067	98958
9 AM	72779	00666	08524	23094	99025
10 AM	72805	00675	08535	23127	99064
11 AM	72853	00693	08544	23159	99129
12 NOON	72947	00718	08621	23240	99200
1 PM	73124	00796	08794	23394	99348
2 PM	73430	00958	09039	23660	99625
3 PM	74005	01366	09572	24161	00169
4 PM	74925	02032	10309	24961	00905
5 PM	76002	02906	11261	25898	01876
6 PM	77202	03873	12360	27010	03018
7 PM	78385	04953	13470	28128	04155
8 PM	79500	05847	14467	29137	05172
9 PM	80571	06705	15459	30126	06177

6. From the information given it is MOST probable that the
   A. most used stairway from the street is nearest turnstile #4
   B. #3 turnstile has just recently been put back in service
   C. entrance stairways are farthest from turnstiles #2, #3, and
      #4
   D. change booth is nearest turnstile #5

7. One of the listed turnstile readings which should be unlikely to
   appear on the regular Combined Railroad Clerks Daily Fare Report
   is
   A. 00602   B. 08437   C. 73430   D. 99625

8. If turnstiles Nos. 3 and 4 had been closed during the entire period of the above tabulation while the total passenger traffic remained the same, and the passengers that would have used turnstiles Nos. 3 and 4 were divided equally among the other three turnstiles, the reading of turnstile #2 at 9 P.M. would have been
   A. 8390   B. 10860   C. 11462   D. 14271

9. If 40% of the passengers entering through these turnstiles on August 5th were registered in the six hours from 3 P.M. to 9 P.M., the total number of passengers registered this day was APPROXIMATELY
   A. 74500   B. 76000   C. 78000   D. 79500

10. The average number of passengers per minute using turnstile #2 during the busiest hour was NEAREST to
    A. 17   B. 18   C. 19   D. 20

11. The total number of passengers using turnstile #2 during the period from 5 P.M. to 8 P.M. was NEAREST to the number of passengers using turnstile
    A. #4 from 1 P.M. to 5 P.M.
    B. #3 from 8 A.M. to 5 P.M.
    C. #1 from 4 P.M. to 7 P.M.
    D. #5 from 4 P.M. to 7 P.M.

Questions 12-14.

DIRECTIONS: Questions 12 through 14 are based on the situation described below. Consider the facts given in this situation when answering these questions.

SITUATION

A new detergent that is to be added to water and the resulting mixture just wiped on any surface has been tested by the station department and appeared to be excellent. However you notice, after inspecting a large number of stations that your porters have cleaned with this detergent, that the surfaces cleaned are not as clean as they formerly were when the old method was used.

12. The MAIN reason for the station department testing the new detergent in the first place was to make certain that
    A. it was very simple to use
    B. a little bit would go a long way
    C. there was no stronger detergent on the market
    D. it was superior to anything formerly used

13. The MAIN reason that such a poor cleaning job resulted was MOST likely due to the
    A. porters being lax on the job
    B. detergent not being as good as expected
    C. incorrect amount of water being mixed with the detergent
    D. fact that the surfaces cleaned needed to be scrubbed

14. The reason for inspecting a number of stations was to
    A. determine whether all porters did the same job
    B. insure that the result of the cleaning job was the same
       in each location
    C. be certain that the detergent was used in each station
       inspected
    D. see whether certain surfaces cleaned better than others

15. A passenger asks you, the assistant supervisor, for directions
    on how to get to a certain place on the transit system. If you
    do not know the answer you should tell the passenger
    A. that you do not know and try to direct him to someone who
       does know
    B. to look the answer up on the subway map posted at the
       station
    C. that only railroad clerks are able to give such directions
    D. to get aboard the next train and to ask the conductor

16. The Employee Suggestion Plan is beneficial to transit authority
    employees because they
    A. become more efficient employees after making a suggestion
    B. are certain to be rewarded for making suggestions
    C. have an opportunity to express their ideas with management
    D. acquaint themselves with the ideas of fellow employees

17. The LEAST valuable source of information for improvements in
    bagging procedures is
    A. suggestions of employees
    B. recommendations from the auditing department
    C. assistant supervisor's records
    D. the Authority's Rules and Regulations

18. A railroad clerk working 12:00 midnight to 8:00 A.M. is directed
    to report to the NYCTA medical staff for a physical examination
    at 11:00 A.M. of the same day. The pay allowed him for reporting
    will be
    A. 1 hour   B. 2 hours   C. 3 hours   D. 4 hours

Questions 19-22.

DIRECTIONS: Questions 19 through 22 are based on the situation de-
            scribed below. Consider the facts given in this situa-
            tion when answering these questions.

SITUATION

John Doe desiring to get to the Stillwell Avenue Station in
Coney Island boarded a Manhattan bound train at the Continental
Avenue Station in Forest Hills at 11:30 A.M. on a weekday.

19. The total number of lines going to Manhattan from Continental
    Avenue at this time of day is
    A. 2   B. 3   C. 4   D. 5

20. A good transfer point where Doe may change trains to reach his destination is
    A. 59th Street and Lexington Avenue
    B. 34th Street and 6th Avenue
    C. 42nd Street and 8th Avenue
    D. Queens Plaza

21. The train which Doe should board to make the trip in the SHORTEST possible time started from
    A. Continental Avenue   B. 179th Street
    C. 169th Street   D. Parsons Blvd.

22. A train he could have transferred to in order to reach his destination without additional change is
    A. IND 'A' train   B. BMT Brighton Express
    C. BMT West End Express   D. IND 'D' train

23. In making a report of an accident on a stairway from the mezzanine to the street at a subway station, the LEAST important of the following items to include is the
    A. time of day   B. number of steps
    C. date   D. weather

24. Assume that, when you are inspecting one of your assigned stations, you notice a porter who in your opinion is under the influence of liquor. Your proper procedure is to
    A. let the porter wait in the change booth and check his condition again later
    B. have the porter escorted to the medical office immediately
    C. have the porter sign out sick and send him home
    D. have the railroad clerk verify your judgment

25. A porter brings to you, the assistant supervisor, a passenger who insists he wants to file a claim against the transit authority. Your BEST procedure would be to
    A. have the passenger wait while you call the supervisor for instructions
    B. give the passenger an accident report form to fill out
    C. take down the complaint in writing and tell the passenger he will be contacted by an adjuster
    D. direct the passenger to the transit authority claims department

26. A porter on the day trick, who is called in to work four hours in excess ahead of his regular tour of duty will be allowed for his days work a total of
    A. 8 hours plus commensurate time off
    B. 12 hours
    C. 14 hours
    D. 17 hours

14

27. When a controversial order is issued, the BEST way for an assistant station supervisor to pass the order on to his men is to
    A. briefly discuss the controversial parts
    B. state that he expects the order to be strictly obeyed
    C. suggest it need not be strictly followed
    D. invite their comments

28. It was recently announced that the Transit Authority will conduct a course in courtesy and passenger-relations for all railroad clerks and porters in the station department. This course is given MAINLY to
    A. increase subway revenue
    B. assure safety of passengers at all times
    C. improve the quality of service
    D. encourage the public to be more friendly

29. One of your railroad clerks reporting for work on the 7:00 A.M. trick states that he does not feel well. At 8:15 A.M. he claims he is much worse and requests permission to go home. He refuses to go to the medical office and, as he is obviously sick, you allow him to leave. The time that should be charged against his sick leave allowance should be
    A. one full day   B. 3/4 day   C. 1/2 day   D. 1/4 day

30. Bulletin orders are often reissued without change. The MAIN reason for doing this is to
    A. make sure that the order gets posted on all bulletin boards
    B. replace any lost copies of the order
    C. remind station employees that the order is still in effect
    D. save time in making up a new order

KEY (CORRECT ANSWERS)

1.	B	11.	B	21.	B
2.	B	12.	D	22.	D
3.	B	13.	B	23.	B
4.	A	14.	B	24.	B
5.	D	15.	A	25.	D
6.	C	16.	C	26.	C
7.	A	17.	D	27.	A
8.	C	18.	C	28.	C
9.	A	19.	B	29.	B
10.	B	20.	B	30.	C

EXAMINATION SECTION

TEST 1

DIRECTIONS: Each question or incomplete statement is followed by
several suggested answers or completions. Select the
one that *BEST* answers the question or completes the
statement. *PRINT THE LETTER OF THE CORRECT ANSWER IN
THE SPACE AT THE RIGHT.*

Questions 1 — 8.

DIRECTIONS   Questions 1 through 8 inclusive are based on the
Bulletin Order shown below. Refer to this bulletin
order when answering these items.

BULLETIN ORDER NO. 9

Subject: Plugged Turnstiles   January 19, ...

    Railroad clerks, especially those assigned to the midnight tour
of duty, are again warned to be alert when a passenger reports that
his token is stuck in a turnstile which will not let him through. If
no platform man or gateman is available, take the passenger's name and
address without leaving the booth, and request the passenger to pay an
additional fare using one of the other turnstiles. Inform the passenge
that the Authority will reimburse him for actual fare lost.

    Railroad clerks are not to leave booths unattended in such in-
stances, but will telephone the Station Department immediately.

    Railroad clerks should notify the Transit Police Bureau immediatel
of any suspicious acts observed, and are redirected to keep booth doors
locked at all times. Booth doors must be closed and locked when railroad clerks are taking turnstile readings or retrieving tokens.

                                 John Doe,
                                 Superintendent

1. When a passenger reports a stuck turnstile, the railroad   1.___
   clerk should telephone the
   A. Superintendent   B. Authority
   C. Transit Police Bureau   D. Station Department

2. The total number of times that the title "railroad clerks"   2.___
   appears in the entire bulletin is
   A. 3   B. 4   C. 5   D. 6

3. When a passenger reports that a token is stuck in a   3.___
   turnstile, the railroad clerk should
   A. notify the Transit Police immediately
   B. tell the passenger to look for a gateman
   C. lock his booth and inspect the turnstile
   D. take the passenger's name and address

4. A passenger who properly reports the loss of a token in a   4.___
   plugged turnstile will probably be reimbursed through
   A. a special messenger   B. the railroad clerk
   C. a gateman   D. the regular mail

5. Retrieving tokens, as used in this bulletin, *MOST*   5.___
   probably means
   A. taking out tokens which have been deposited in
      turnstiles
   B. picking up tokens which have dropped to the floor
   C. paying out cash for tokens returned by passengers
   D. counting the number of tokens sold since the
      previous count

6. If railroad clerks at a certain location work in three   6.___
   consecutive 8-hour tours to cover the 24 hours in a day,
   and the A.M. tour finishes at 3:00 P.M., the hours of work
   for the midnight tour are *MOST* likely
   A. 12:00 midnight to 8:00 A.M.
   B. 11:00 P.M. to 7:00 A.M.
   C. 10:00 P.M. to 6:00 A.M.
   D. 9:00 P.M. to 5:00 A.M.

7. If bulletin order number 1 was issued on January 2,   7.___
   bulletins are being issued at the rate of
   A. one a day   B. one a week
   C. one every two days   D. two a week

8. From the statements in this bulletin, it is clear that   8.___
   there *MUST* be
   A. gatemen on duty at every change booth
   B. telephones in all change booths
   C. suspicious characters around every station
   D. platformmen always on duty

KEY (CORRECT ANSWERS)

1.	D
2.	B
3.	D
4.	D
5.	A
6.	B
7.	C
8.	B

TEST 2

Questions 1 - 7.

DIRECTIONS. Questions 1 - 7 are based on the Procedure for Inspection, Repairs, or Alterations to Low Turnstiles given below. Refer to this procedure when answering these items.

PROCEDURE FOR INSPECTION, REPAIRS, OR ALTERATIONS TO LOW TURNSTILES

When a maintainer arrives at a station to repair or inspect a turnstile, the railroad clerk and the maintainer together will take the register reading of the turnstile, and the railroad clerk will record the reading on form TAA-G-458 before any work is begun.

When the work is completed and before the turnstile is opened for service, the railroad clerk and the maintainer together will again take the register reading. The railroad clerk will enter this second reading on form TAA-G-458. The difference between the two readings, representing the number of test registrations made on that turnstile, will also be entered.

The turnstile maintainer shall make a report in duplicate on form TAM-L27 showing the register readings before and after adjustment, and shall have the railroad clerk initial the readings as verification. If test operation is by observation of passengers entering through the turnstile just repaired, the number of such passengers shall be noted in the "Remarks" column. The turnstile maintainer shall also enter the time of start and finish of the work, and on the original copy of the report only, the type of inspection or work done.

The railroad clerk shall transmit the duplicate of form TAM-L27 together with his form TAA-G-458 to Audit of Passenger Revenue.

1. The number of entries on the maintainer's form TAM-L27   1.___
   that the railroad clerk is required to initial for each
   turnstile worked on is
   A. 1   B. 2   C. 3   D. 4

2. The number of entries that the railroad clerk is required   2.___
   to make on form TAA-G-458 is
   A. 1   B. 2   C. 3   D. 4

3. In accordance with the foregoing, the number of copies of   3.___
   form TAA-G-458 that *MUST* be made out by the railroad
   clerk is
   A. 4   B. 3   C. 2   D. 1

4. With respect to form TAM-L27, the letters TA *MOST* likely stand for   4.___
    A. transit authority   B. token adjustment
    C. turnstile alteration   D. time account

5. The form of test operation specifically mentioned in the   5.___
procedure is by
    A. use of special counters
    B. observation of passengers entering
    C. use of a stated number of tokens
    D. changing the register reading

6. It is stated in the procedure that the maintainer should   6.___
enter in the "Remarks" column of form TAM-L27 the
    A. initial register reading
    B. number of test registrations
    C. number of passengers involved in test registrations
    D. final register reading

7. The information that is *NOT* included when the railroad   7.___
clerk transmits the two forms to Audit of Passenger
Revenue is the
    A. final turnstile reading
    B. type of work done
    C. number of test registrations
    D. number of test operations made by passengers entering

KEY (CORRECT ANSWERS)

1. B
2. C
3. D
4. A
5. B
6. C
7. B

TEST 3

DIRECTIONS: Each question or incomplete statement is followed by several suggested answers or completions. Select the one that *BEST* answers the question or completes the statement. *PRINT THE LETTER OF THE CORRECT ANSWER IN THE SPACE AT THE RIGHT.*

Questions 1 - 8.

DIRECTIONS: Questions 1 through 8 are based on the paragraphs about accident statistics given below. Read these statistics carefully before answering these questions.

ACCIDENT STATISTICS

Accidents are among our nation's leading killers, maulers, and money wasters. In the United States during 1985, according to the National Safety Council figures, there were 100,000 fatal accidents of all kinds, and ten million various types of disabling injuries. Some 40,000 deaths involved motor vehicles. The home accounted for 29,000 fatalities, and public places 17,000. There were 14,000 deaths and two million disabling injuries in industry.

In 1985, the total cost of accidents in the United States was at least 16 billion dollars. For industry alone, the cost of accidents was 5 billion dollars, equal to $70 per worker. The total time lost was about 230 million man days of work.

1. The statistics quoted above are for   1.___
   A. the home only   B. the entire United States
   C. New York State   D. New York City

2. The statistics quoted above are for the year   2.___
   A. 1978   B. 1980   C. 1983   D. 1985

3. Of the 100,000 fatal accidents of all kinds, those *NOT*   3.___
   involved with motor vehicles totaled
   A. 17,000   B. 29,000   C. 40,000   D. 60,000

4. The number of disabling injuries of all kinds which were   4.___
   listed for industry was
   A. 10 million   B. 8 million   C. 4 million   D. 2 million

5. Accidents cost our nation at *LEAST*   5.___
   A. 16 billion dollars   B. 5 billion dollars
   C. 10 million dollars   D. 2 million dollars

6. The number of deaths due to accidents in the home was   6.___
   close to
   A. 15,000   B. 20,000   C. 30,000   D. 40,000

7. The number of deaths per day from accidents of all kinds   7.___
   averaged about
   A. 275   B. 300   C. 325   D. 350

8. During the year for which these statistics are given,   8.___
   the cost of industrial accidents per worker was
   A. $230   B. $70   C. $17   D. $5

KEY (CORRECT ANSWERS)

1. B
2. B
3. D
4. D
5. A
6. C
7. A
8. B

———

TEST 4

DIRECTIONS· Each question or incomplete statement is followed by several suggested answers or completions. Select the one that *BEST* answers the question or completes the statement. *PRINT THE LETTER OF THE CORRECT ANSWER IN THE SPACE AT THE RIGHT.*

Questions 1 - 6.

DIRECTIONS: Questions 1 through 6 are based on the Bulletin Order given below. Refer to this bulletin order when answering these questions.

BULLETIN ORDER NO. 67

SUBJECT: Procedure for Handling Fire Occurrences   6-17---

In order that the Fire Department may be notified of all fires, even those that have been extinguished by our own employees, any employee having knowledge of a fire must notify the Station Department Office immediately on telephone extensions: D-4177, D-4181, D-4185, or D-4189.

Specific information regarding the fire should include the location of the fire, the approximate distance north or south of the nearest station, and the track designation, line and division.

In addition, the report should contain information as to the status of the fire and whether our forces have extinguished it or if Fire Department equipment is needed.

When all information has been obtained, the Station Supervisor in Charge in the Station Department Office will notify the Desk Trainmaster of the Division involved.

Richard Roe,
Superintendent

1. An employee having knowledge of a fire should first notify the   1.___
   A. Station Department Office   B. Fire Department
   C. Desk Trainmaster   D. Station Supervisor

2. If bulletin order number 1 was issued on January 2, bulletins are being issued at the monthly average of   2.___
   A. 8   B. 10   C. 12   D. 14

3. It is clear from the bulletin that   3.___
   A. employees are expected to be expert fire fighters
   B. many fires occur on the transit system
   C. train service is usually suspended whenever a fire occurs
   D. some fires are extinguished without the help of the Fire Department

4. From the information furnished in this bulletin, it can   4.___
be assumed that the
  A. Station Department office handles a considerable
     number of telephone calls
  B. Superintendent investigates the handling of all
     subway fires
  C. Fire Department is notified only in case of large
     fires
  D. employee first having knowledge of the fire must
     call all 4 extensions

5. The probable reason for notifying the Fire Department   5.___
even when the fire has been extinguished by a subway
employee is because the Fire Department is
  A. a city agency
  B. still responsible to check the fire
  C. concerned with fire prevention
  D. required to clean up after the fire

6. Information about the fire *NOT* specifically required is   6.___
  A. track   B. time of day
  C. station   D. division

KEY (CORRECT ANSWERS)

1. A
2. C
3. D
4. A
5. C
6. B

TEST 5

DIRECTIONS: Each question or incomplete statement is followed by several suggested answers or completions. Select the one that *BEST* answers the question or completes the statement. *PRINT THE LETTER OF THE CORRECT ANSWER IN THE SPACE AT THE RIGHT.*

Questions 1 - 4.

DIRECTIONS: Questions 1 through 4 are based on the regulations relating to voting on Primary Day as given below. Read these regulations carefully before answering these items.

REGULATIONS RELATING TO VOTING ON PRIMARY DAY

The polls are open from 3:00 to 10:00 P.M. Employees who are on duty Primary Day during the period polls are open, and who would not have two consecutive hours free time to vote, will be granted leave of absence for two hours without loss of pay.

Examples·
1. Employees reporting for work at 3 PM to and including 4:59 PM, will be allowed two hours leave with pay.
2. Employees who report to work at 5 PM or thereafter, no time to be allowed.
3. Employees who complete their tour of duty and are cleared on or before 8 PM, no time to be allowed.

1. A two-hour leave of absence with pay will be granted to employees who are on duty Primary Day if they   1.____
   A. have to work two hours while the polls are open
   B. would not have two consecutive hours free time to vote
   C. are working a day tour
   D. are working a night tour

2. An employee working an evening tour will be allowed two hours with pay if he has to report for work at   2.____
   A. 3:00 PM   B. 5:00 PM   C. 7:00 PM   D. 9:00 PM

3. An employee working an afternoon tour will be allowed two hours with pay if he clears at   3.____
   A. 6:00 PM   B. 7:00 PM   C. 8:00 PM   D. 9:00 PM

4. An employee working an afternoon tour will *NOT* be allowed any time off if he clears at   4.____
   A. 8:00 PM   B. 8:30 PM   C. 9:30 PM   D. 10:00 PM

KEY (CORRECT ANSWERS)

1. B
2. A
3. D
4. A

SUPERVISION, ADMINISTRATION, MANAGEMENT AND ORGANIZATION
EXAMINATION SECTION

DIRECTIONS FOR THIS SECTION:
Each question or incomplete statement is followed by several suggested answers or completions. Select the one that BEST answers the question or completes the statement. *PRINT THE LETTER OF THE CORRECT ANSWER IN THE SPACE AT THE RIGHT.*

TEST 1

1. The one of the following practices by a supervisor which is *most likely* to lead to confusion and inefficiency is for him to
    A. give orders verbally directly to the man assigned to the job
    B. issue orders only in writing
    C. follow up his orders after issuing them
    D. relay his orders to the men through co-workers   1. ...

2. If you are given an oral order by a supervisor which you do not understand completely, you should
    A. use your own judgment
    B. discuss the order with your men
    C. ask your superior for a further explanation
    D. carry out that part of the order which you do understand and then ask for more information   2. ...

3. An orientation program for a group of new employees should NOT *ordinarily* include a
    A. review of the organizational structure of the agency
    B. detailed description of the duties of each new employee
    C. description of the physical layout of the repair shop
    D. statement of the rules pertaining to sick leave, vacation, and holidays   3. ...

4. The MOST important rule to follow with regard to discipline is that a man should be disciplined
    A. after everyone has had time to "cool off"
    B. as soon as possible after the infraction of rules
    C. only for serious rule violations
    D. before he makes a mistake   4. ...

5. If the men under your supervision continue to work effectively even when you are out sick for several days, it would *most probably* indicate that
    A. the men are merely trying to show you up
    B. the men are in constant fear of you and are glad you are away
    C. you have trained your men properly and have their full cooperation
    D. you are serving no useful purpose since the men can get along without you   5. ...

6. When evaluating subordinates, the employee who should be rated HIGHEST by his supervisor is the one who
    A. never lets the supervisor do heavy lifting
    B. asks many questions about the work
    C. makes many suggestions on work procedures
    D. listens to instructions and carries them out   6. ...

7. Of the following, the factor which is *generally* MOST im-   7. ...
   portant to the conduct of successful training is
     A. time   B. preparation   C. equipment   D. space

8. One of the MAJOR disadvantages of "on-the-job" training   8. ...
   is that it
     A. requires a long training period for instructors
     B. may not be progressive
     C. requires additional equipment
     D. may result in the waste of supplies

9. For a supervisor to train workers in several trades which   9. ...
   involve various skills, presents many training problems.
   The one of the following which is NOT true in such a training situation is that
     A. less supervision is required
     B. greater planning for training is required
     C. rotation of assignments is necessary
     D. less productivity can be expected

10. For a supervisor of repair workers to have each worker   10. ...
    specialize in learning a single trade is, *generally*,
      A. *desirable;* each worker will become expert in his as-
        signed trade
      B. *undesirable;* there is less flexibility of assignments
        possible when each worker has learned only a single
        trade
      C. *desirable;* the training responsibility of the super-
        visor is simplified when each worker is required to
        learn a single trade
      D. *undesirable;* workers lose interest quickly when they
        know they are expected to learn a single trade

11. An IMPORTANT advantage of standardizing work procedures   11. ...
    is that it
      A. develops all-around skills
      B. makes the work less monotonous
      C. provides an incentive for good work
      D. enables the work to be done with less supervision

12. Generally, the GREATEST difficulty in introducing new   12. ...
    work methods is due to the fact that
      A. men become set in their ways
      B. the old way is generally better
      C. only the department will benefit from changes
      D. explaining new methods is time consuming

13. Assume that you are required to transmit an order, with   13. ...
    which you do not agree, to your subordinates. In this
    case, it would be BEST for you to
      A. ask one of your superiors to transmit the order
      B. refuse to transmit an order with which you do not agree
      C. transmit the order but be sure to explain that you do
        not agree with it
      D. transmit the order and enforce it to the best of your
        ability

14. The MAIN reason for written orders is that   14. ...
      A. proper blame can be placed if the order is not car-
        ried out
      B. the order will be carried out faster
      C. the order can be properly analyzed as to its meaning
      D. there will be no doubt as to what the order says

15. You have been informed unofficially by another shop man-   15. ...
    ager that some of the men under your supervision are loaf-
    ing on the job. This situation can be BEST handled by
       A. telling the man to mind his own business
       B. calling the men together and reprimanding them
       C. having the men work under your direct supervision
       D. arranging to make spot checks at more frequent in-
          tervals
16. Suggestions on improving methods of doing work, when sub-   16. ...
    mitted by a new employee, should be
       A. examined for possible merit because the new man may
          have a fresh viewpoint
       B. ignored because it would make the old employees re-
          sentful
       C. disregarded because he is too unfamiliar with the work
       D. examined only for the purpose of judging the new man
17. One of your employees often slows down the work of his   17. ...
    crew by playing practical jokes. The BEST way to handle
    this situation is to
       A. arrange for his assignment to more than his share of
          unpleasant jobs
       B. warn him that he must stop this practice at once
       C. ignore this situation for he will soon tire of it
       D. ask your superior to transfer him
18. One of your men is always complaining about working con-   18. ...
    ditions, equipment, and his fellow workers. The BEST
    action for you to take in this situation is to
       A. have this man work alone if possible
       B. consider each complaint on its merits
       C. tell him bluntly that you will not listen to any of
          his complaints
       D. give this man the worst jobs until he quits complaining
19. It is generally agreed that men who are interested in   19. ...
    their work will do the best work. A supervisor can *least*
    stimulate this interest by
       A. complimenting men on good work
       B. correcting men on their working procedures
       C. striving to create overtime for his men
       D. recommending merit raises for excellent work
20. If you, as a supervisor, have criticized one of your men   20. ...
    for making a mistake, you should
       A. remind the man of his error from time to time to keep
          him on his toes
       B. overlook any further errors which this man may make,
          otherwise he may feel he is a victim of discrimination
       C. give the man the opportunity to redeem himself
       D. impress the man with the fact that all his work will
          be closely checked from then on
21. In his efforts to maintain standards of performance, a   21. ...
    shop manager uses a system of close supervision to detect
    or catch errors. An *opposite* method of accomplishing the
    same objective is to employ a program which
       A. instills in each employee a pride of workmanship to
          do the job correctly the first time
       B. groups each job according to the importance to the
          overall objectives of the program

3

    C. makes the control of quality the responsibility of an
       inspector
    D. emphasizes that there is a "one" best way for an em-
       ployee to do a specific job

22. Assume that after taking over a repair shop, a shop man-   22. ...
    ager feels that he is taking too much time maintaining
    records. He should
    A. temporarily assign this job to one of his senior
       repair crew chiefs
    B. get together with his supervisor to determine if all
       these records are needed
    C. stop keeping those records which he believes are un-
       necessary
    D. spend a few additional hours each day until his records
       are current

23. In order to apply performance standards to employees en-   23. ...
    gaged in repair shop activities, a shop manager must FIRST
    A. allow workers to decide for themselves the way to do
       the job
    B. determine what is acceptable as satisfactory work
    C. separate the more difficult tasks from the simpler
       tasks
    D. stick to an established work schedule

24. Of the following actions a shop manager can take to deter-   24. ...
    mine whether the vehicles used in his shop are being uti-
    lized properly, the one which will give him the *least*
    meaningful information is
    A. conducting an analysis of vehicle assignments
    B. reviewing the number of miles travelled by each
       vehicle with and without loads
    C. recording the unloaded weights of each vehicle
    D. comparing the amount of time vehicles are parked at
       job sites with the time required to travel to and
       from job sites

25. For a shop manager, the MOST important reason that equip-   25. ...
    ment which is used infrequently should be considered for
    disposal is that
    A. the time required for its maintenance could be better
       used elsewhere
    B. such equipment may cause higher management to think
       that your shop is not busy
    C. the men may resent having to work on such equipment
    D. such equipment usually has a higher breakdown rate
       in operation

TEST 2

1. Assume that one of your subordinates approaches you with   1. ...
    a grievance concerning working conditions. Of the follow-
    ing, the BEST action for you to take *first* is to
    A. "soft-soap" him, since most grievances are imaginary
    B. settle the grievance to his satisfaction
    C. try to talk him out of his complaint
    D. listen patiently and sincerely to the complaint

2. Of the following, the BEST way for a supervisor to help a   2. ...
   subordinate learn a new skill which requires the use of
   tools is for him to give this subordinate
      A. a list of good books on the subject
      B. lectures on the theoretical aspects of the task
      C. opportunities to watch someone using the tools
      D. opportunities to practice the skill, under close
         supervision

3. A supervisor finds that his own work load is excessive   3. ...
   because several of his subordinates are unable to complete
   their assignments.
   Of the following, the BEST action for him to take to improve this situation is to
      A. discipline these subordinates
      B. work overtime   C. request additional staff
      D. train these subordinates in more efficient work methods

4. The one of the following situations which is MOST likely   4. ...
   to be the result of *poor* morale is a(n)
      A. high rate of turnover
      B. decrease in number of requests by subordinates for
         transfers
      C. increase in the backlog of work
      D. decrease in the rate of absenteeism

5. As a supervisor, you find that several of your subordinates 5. ...
   are not meeting their deadlines because they are doing work
   assigned to them by one of your fellow supervisors without
   your knowledge.
   Of the following, the BEST course of action for you to take
   in this situation is to
      A. tell the other supervisors to make future assignments
         through you
      B. assert your authority by publicly telling the other
         supervisors to stop issuing orders to your workers
      C. go along with this practice; it is an effective way
         to fully utilize the available manpower
      D. take the matter directly to your immediate supervisor
         without delay

6. If a supervisor of a duplicating section in an agency hears 6. ...
   a rumor concerning a change in agency personnel policy
   through the "grapevine," he should
      A. repeat it to his subordinates so they will be informed
      B. not repeat it to his subordinates before he determines
         the facts because, as supervisor, his work may give it
         unwarranted authority
      C. repeat it to his subordinates so that they will like
         him for confiding in them
      D. not repeat it to his subordinates before he determines
         the facts because a duplicating section is not con-
         cerned with matters of policy

7. When teaching a new employee how to operate a machine, a   7. ...
   supervisor should FIRST
      A. let the employee try to operate the machine by him-
         self, since he can learn only by his mistakes
      B. explain the process to him with the use of diagrams
         before showing him the machine

  C. have him memorize the details of the operation from
    the manual
  D. explain and demonstrate the various steps in the proc-
    ess, making sure he understands each step

8. If a subordinate accuses you of always giving him the least   8. ...
 desirable assignments, you should *immediately*
  A. tell him that it is not true and you do not want to
    hear any more about it
  B. try to get specific details from him, so that you
    can find out what his impressions are based on
  C. tell him that you distribute assignments in the
    fairest way possible and he must be mistaken
  D. ask him what current assignment he has that he does
    not like, and assign it to someone else

9. Suppose that the production of an operator under your su-   9. ...
 pervision has been unsatisfactory and you have decided to
 have a talk with him about it.
 During the interview, it would be BEST for you to
  A. discuss *only* the subordinate's weak points so that he
    can overcome them
  B. discuss *only* the subordinate's strong points so that
    he will not become discouraged
  C. compare the subordinate's work with that of his co-
    workers so that he will know what is expected of him
  D. discuss *both* his weak and strong points so that he
    will get a view of his overall performance

10. Suppose that an operator under your supervision makes a   10. ...
 mistake in color on a 2,000-page job and runs it on white
 paper instead of on blue paper.
 Of the following, your BEST course in these circumstances
 would be to point out the error to the operator *and*
  A. have the operator rerun the job immediately on blue
    paper
  B. send the job to the person who ordered it without
    comment
  C. send the job to the person who ordered it and tell
    him it could not be done on blue paper
  D. ask the person who ordered the job whether the white
    paper is acceptable

11. Assuming that all your subordinates have equal technical   11. ...
 competence, the BEST policy for a supervisor to follow
 when making assignments of undesirable jobs would be to
  A. distribute them as evenly as possible among his
    subordinates
  B. give them to the subordinate with the poorest attend-
    ance record
  C. ask the subordinate with the least seniority to do them
  D. assign them to the subordinate who is least likely to
    complain

12. To get the BEST results when training a number of subor-   12. ...
 dinates at the *same* time, a supervisor should
  A. treat all of them in an identical manner to avoid ac-
    cusations of favoritism
  B. treat them all fairly, but use different approaches
    in dealing with people of different personality types

C. train only one subordinate, and have him train the others, because this will save a lot of the supervisor's time

D. train first the subordinates who learn quickly so as to make the others think that the operation is easy to learn

13. Assume that, after a week's vacation, you return to find that one of your subordinates has produced a job which is unsatisfactory.
Your BEST course of action at *that* time would be to
A. talk to your personnel department about implementing disciplinary action
B. discuss unsatisfactory work in the unit at a meeting with all of your subordinates
C. discuss the job with the subordinate to determine why he was unable to do it properly
D. ignore the matter, because it is too late to correct the mistake

13. ...

14. Suppose that an operator under your supervision informs you that Mr. Y, a senior administrator in your agency, has been submitting for xeroxing many papers which are obviously personal in nature. The operator wants to know what to do about it, since the duplication of personal papers is against agency rules.
Your BEST course in these circumstances would be to
A. tell the operator to pretend not to notice the content of the material and continue to xerox whatever is given to him
B. tell the operator that Mr. Y, as a senior administrator, must have gotten special permission to have personal papers duplicated
C. have the operator refer Mr. Y to you and inform Mr. Y yourself that duplication of personal papers is against agency rules
D. call Mr. Y's superior and tell him that Mr. Y has been having personal papers duplicated, which is against agency rules

14. ...

15. Assume that you are teaching a certain process to an operator under your supervision.
In order to BEST determine whether he is *actually* learning what you are teaching, you should ask questions which
A. can easily be answered by a "yes" or "no"
B. require or encourage guessing
C. require a short description of what has been taught
D. are somewhat ambiguous so as to make the learner think about the procedures in question

15. ...

16. If an employee is chronically late or absent, as his supervisor, it would be BEST for you to
A. let his work pile up so he can see that no one else will do it for him
B. discuss the matter with him and stress the importance of finding a solution
C. threaten to enter a written report on the matter into his personnel file
D. work out a system with him so he can have a different work schedule than the other employees

16. ...

7

17. Assume that you have a subordinate who has just finished a basic training course in the operation of a machine. Giving him a large and difficult *first* assignment would be
    A. *good*, because it would force him to "learn the ropes"
    B. *bad*, because he would probably have difficulty in carrying it out, discouraging him and resulting in a waste of time and supplies
    C. *good*, because how he handles it would give you an excellent basis for judging his competence
    D. *bad*, because he would probably assume that you are discriminating against him

17. ...

18. After putting a new employee under your supervision through an initial training period, assigning him to work with a more experienced employee for a while would be a
    A. *good idea*, because it would give him the opportunity to observe what he had been taught and to participate in production himself
    B. *bad idea*, because he should not be required to work under the direction of anyone who is not his supervisor
    C. *good idea*, because it would raise the morale of the more experienced employee who could use him to do all the unpleasant chores
    D. *bad idea*, because the best way for him to learn would be to give him full responsibility for assignments right away

18. ...

19. Assume that a supervisor is responsible for ordering supplies for the duplicating section in his agency.
    Which one of the following actions would be MOST helpful in determining *when* to place orders so that an adequate supply of materials will be on hand at all times?
    A. Taking an inventory of supplies on hand at least every two months
    B. Asking his subordinvtes to inform him when they see that supplies are low
    C. Checking the inventory of supplies whenever he has time
    D. Keeping a running inventory of supplies and a record of estimated needs

19. ...

20. Routine procedures that have worked well in the past should be reviewed periodically by a supervisor MAINLY because
    A. they may have become outdated or in need of revision
    B. employees might dislike the procedures even though they have proven successful in the past
    C. these reviews are the main part of a supervisor's job
    D. this practice serves to give the supervisor an idea of how productive his subordinates are

20. ...

21. Assume that an employee tells his supervisor about a grievance he has against a co-worker. The supervisor assures the employee that he will immediately take action to eliminate the grievance.
    The supervisor's attitude should be considered
    A. *correct;* because a good supervisor is one who can come to a quick decision

21. ...

8

    B. *incorrect;* because the supervisor should have told the employee that he will investigate the grievance and then determine a future course of action

    C. *correct;* because the employee's morale will be higher, resulting in greater productivity

    D. *incorrect;* because the supervisor should remain un-involved and let the employees settle grievances between themselves

22. If an employee's work output is low and of poor quality due to faulty work habits, the MOST constructive of the following ways for a supervisor to correct this situation, *generally,* is to   22. ...

    A. discipline the employee

    B. transfer the employee to another unit

    C. provide additional training

    D. check the employee's work continuously

23. Assume that it becomes necessary for a supervisor to ask his staff to work overtime. Which one of the following techniques is MOST likely to win their willing cooperation to do this?   23. ...

    A. Explain that this is part of their job specification entitled, "performs related work"

    B. Explain the reason it is necessary for the employees to work overtime

    C. Promise the employees special consideration regarding future leave matters

    D. Explain that if the employees do not work overtime, they will face possible disciplinary action

24. If an employee's work performance has recently fallen below established minimum standards for quality and quantity, the threat of demotion or other disciplinary measures as an attempt to improve this employee's performance would *probably* be the MOST acceptable and effective course of action   24. ...

    A. *only* after other more constructive measures have failed

    B. *if* applied uniformly to all employees as soon as performance falls below standard

    C. *only* if the employee understands that the threat will not actually be carried out

    D. *if* the employee is promised that as soon as his work performance improves, he will be reinstated to his previous status

25. If, as a supervisor, it becomes necessary for you to assign an employee to supervise your unit during your vacation, it would *generally* be BEST to select the employee who   25. ...

    A. is the best technician on the staff

    B. can get the work out smoothly, without friction

    C. has the most seniority

    D. is the most popular with the group

TEST 3

1. An employee under your supervision has demonstrated a deep-seated personality problem that has begun to affect his work. This situation should be   1. ...

    A. *ignored*; mainly because such problems usually resolve
themselves
    B. *handled*; mainly because the employee should be assisted
in seeking professional help
    C. *ignored*; mainly because the employee will consider any
advice as interference
    D. *handled*; mainly because supervisors should be quali-
fied to resolve deep-seated personality problems

2. Of the following, a supervisor will usually be MOST suc-   2. ...
cessful in maintaining employee morale while providing
effective leadership if he
    A. takes prompt disciplinary action every time it is
needed
    B. gives difficult assignments only to those workers
who ask for such work
    C. promises his workers anything reasonable they request
    D. relies entirely on his staff for decisions

3. When a supervisor makes an assignment to his subordinates,   3. ...
he should include a clear statement of what results are
expected when the assignment is completed.
Of the following, the BEST reason for following this procedure is that it will
    A. make it unnecessary for the supervisor to check on the
progress of the work
    B. stimulate initiative and cooperation on the part of
the more responsible workers
    C. give the subordinates a way to judge whether their
work is meeting the requirements
    D. give the subordinates the feeling that they have some
freedom of action

4. Assume that, on a new employee's first day of work, his   4. ...
supervisor gives him a good orientation by telling him the
general regulations and procedures used in the office and
introducing him to his department head and fellow employees.
For the remainder of the day, it would be BEST for the supervisor to
    A. give him steady instruction in all phases of his job,
while stressing its most important aspects
    B. have him observe a fellow employee perform the duties
of the job
    C. instruct him in that part of the job which he would
prefer to learn first
    D. give him a simple task which requires little instruc-
tion and allows him to familiarize himself with the
surroundings

5. When it becomes necessary to criticize subordinates because   5. ...
several errors in the unit's work have been discovered, the
supervisor should *usually*
    A. focus on the job operation and avoid placing personal
blame
    B. make every effort to fix blame and admonish the person
responsible
    C. include in the criticism those employees who recognize
and rectify their own mistakes
    D. repeat the criticism at regular intervals in order to
impress the subordinates with the seriousness of their
errors

6. If two employees under your supervision are continually   6. ...
   bickering and cannot get along together, the FIRST action
   that you should take is to
     A. investigate possible ways of separating them
     B. ask your immediate superior for the procedure to fol-
        low in this situation
     C. determine the cause of their difficulty
     D. develop a plan and tell both parties to try it
7. In general, it is appropriate to recommend the transfer of 7. ...
   an employee for all of the following reasons EXCEPT
     A. rewarding him
     B. providing him with a more challenging job
     C. remedying an error in initial placement
     D. disciplining him
8. Of the following, the MAIN *disadvantage* of basing a train- 8. ...
   ing and development program on a series of lectures is that
   the lecture technique
     A. does not sufficiently involve trainees in the learning
        process
     B. is more costly than other methods of training
     C. cannot be used to facilitate the understanding of dif-
        ficult information
     D. is time consuming and inefficient
9. A supervisor has been assigned to train a new employee who   9. ...
   is properly motivated but has made many mistakes.
   In the interview between the supervisor and employee about
   this problem, the employee should FIRST be
     A. asked if he can think of anything that he can do to
        improve his work
     B. complimented sincerely on some aspect of his work that
        is satisfactory
     C. asked to explain why he made the mistakes
     D. advised that he may be dismissed if he continues to
        be careless
10. In training subordinates for more complex work, a super-   10. ...
    visor must be aware of the progress that the subordinates
    are making.
    Determinination of the results that have been accomplished
    by training is a concept *commonly* known as
      A. reinforcement   B. feedback
      C. cognitivie dissonance D. the halo effect
11. Assume that one of your subordinates loses interest in   11. ...
    his work because he feels that your recent evaluation of
    his performance was unfair.
    The one of the following which is the BEST way to help him
    is to
      A. establish frequent deadlines for his work
      B. discuss his feelings and attitude with him
      C. discuss with him only the positive aspects of his
         performance
      D. arrange for his transfer to another unit
12. Informal organizations often develop at work.   12. ...
    Of the following, the supervisor should realize that
    these groups will USUALLY
      A. determine work pace through unofficial agreements
      B. restrict vital communication channels

11

C. lower morale by providing a chance to spread grievances
D. provide leaders who will substitute for the supervisor when he is absent

13. Assume that you, the supervisor, have called to your of-   13. ...
fice a subordinate whom, on several recent occasions, you
have seen using the office telephone for personal use.
In this situation, it would be MOST appropriate to *begin*
the interview by
    A. discussing the disciplinary action that you believe
       to be warranted
    B. asking the subordinate to explain the reason for his
       personal use of the office telephone
    C. telling the subordinate about other employees who were
       disciplined for the same offense
    D. informing the subordinate that he is not to use the
       office telephone under any circumstances until further
       notice

14. Of the following, the success of any formal training pro-   14. ...
gram depends PRIMARILY upon the
    A. efficient and thorough preparation of materials,
       facilities, and procedures for instruction
    B. training program's practical relevance to the on-the-
       job situation
    C. scheduling of training sessions so as to minimize
       interference with normal job responsibilities
    D. creation of a positive initial reception on the part
       of the trainees

15. All of the following are legitimate purposes for regular-   15. ...
ly evaluating employee performance EXCEPT
    A. stimulating improvement in performance
    B. developing more accurate standards to be used in
       future ratings
    C. encouraging a spirit of competition
    D. allowing the employee to set realistic work goals
       for himself

16. A certain supervisor is very conscientious. He wants to   16. ...
receive personally all reports, correspondence, etc., and
to be completely involved in all of the unit's operations.
However, he is having difficulty in keeping up with the
growing amount of paperwork.
Of the following, the MOST desirable course of action for
him to take is to
    A. put in more hours on the job
    B. ask for additional office help
    C. begin to delegate more of his work
    D. inquire of his supervisor if the paper work is really
       necessary

17. Assume that you are a supervisor. One of the workers   17. ...
under your supervision expresses his need to speak to you
about a client who has been particularly uncooperative in
providing information.
The MOST appropriate action for you to take FIRST would be
to
    A. agree to see the client for the worker in order to get
       the information

12

    B. advise the worker to try several more times to get
       the information before he asks you for help
    C. tell the worker you will go with him to see the
       client in order to observe his technique
    D. ask the worker some questions in order to determine
       the type of help he needs in this situation

18. The supervisor who is MOST likely to achieve a high level   18. ...
    of productivity from the professional employees under his
    supervision is the *one* who
    A. watches their progress continuously
    B. provides them with just enough information to carry
       out their assigned tasks
    C. occasionally pitches in and helps them with their work
    D. shares with them responsibility for setting work goals

19. Assume that there has been considerable friction for some   19. ...
    time among the workers of a certain unit. The supervisor
    in charge of this unit becomes aware that the problem is
    getting serious as shown by increased absenteeism and late-
    ness, loud arguments, etc.
    Of the following, the BEST course of action for the super-
    visor to take FIRST is to
    A. have a staff discussion about objectives and problems
    B. seek out and penalize the apparent trouble-makers
    C. set up and enforce stricter formal rules
    D. discipline the next subordinate who causes friction

20. Assume that an employee under your supervision asks you   20. ...
    for some blank paper and pencils to take home to her young
    grandson who, she says, delights in drawing.
    The one of the following actions you SHOULD take is to
    A. give her the material she wants and refrain from any
       comment
    B. refuse her request and tell her that the use of of-
       fice supplies for personal reasons is not proper
    C. give her the material but suggest that she buy it
       next time
    D. tell her to take the material herself since you do
       not want to know anything about this matter

21. A certain supervisor is given a performance evaluation by   21. ...
    his superior.
    In it he is commended for his method of "delegation," a
    term that USUABLY refers to the action of
    A. determining the priorities for activities which must
       be completed
    B. assigning to subordinates some of the duties for which
       he is responsible
    C. standardizing operations in order to achieve results
       as close as possible to established goals
    D. dividing the activities necessary to achieve an ob-
       jective into simple steps

22. A supervisor is approached by a subordinate who complains   22. ...
    that a fellow worker is not assuming his share of the
    workload and is, therefore, causing more work for others
    in the office.
    Of the following, the MOST appropriate action for the su-
    pervisor to take in response to this complaint is to tell
    the subordinate

   A. that he will look into the matter
   B. to concentrate on his own job and not to worry about others
   C. to discuss the matter with the other worker
   D. that not everyone is capable of working at the same pace

23. Aside from the formal relationships established by manage-   23. ...
ment, informal and unofficial relationships will be developed among the personnel within an organization.
Of the following, the MAIN importance of such informal
relationships to the operations of the formal organization
is that they
   A. reinforce the basic goals of the formal organization
   B. insure the interchangeability of the personnel within
the organization
   C. provide an additional channel of communications within the formal organization
   D. insure predictability and control of the behavior of
members of the organization

24. The most productive worker in a unit frequently takes   24. ...
overly-long coffee breaks and lunch hours while maintaining his above-average rate of productivity.
Of the following, it would be MOST advisable for the supervisor to
   A. reprimand him, because rules must be enforced equally
regardless of the merit of an individual's job performance
   B. ignore the infractions because a superior worker
should be granted extra privileges for his efforts
   C. take no action unless others in the unit complain,
because a reprimand may hurt the superior worker's
feelings and cause him to produce less
   D. tell other members of the unit that a comparable rate
of productivity on their part will be rewarded with
similar privileges

25. A supervisor has been asked by his superior to choose an   25. ...
employee to supervise a special project.
Of the following, the MOST significant factor to consider
in making this choice is the employee's
   A. length of service   B. ability to do the job
   C. commitment to the goals of the agency
   D. attitude toward his fellow workers

TEST 4

1. Assume that you are a newly appointed supervisor.   1. ...
Your MOST important responsibility is to
   A. make certain that all of the employees under your
supervision are treated equally
   B. reduce disciplinary situations to a minimum
   C. insure an atmosphere of mutual trust between your
workers and yourself
   D. see that the required work is done properly

2. In order to make sure that work is completed on time, the   2. ...
supervisor should

    A. pitch in and do as much of the work herself as she can
    B. schedule the work and control its progress
    C. not assign more than one person to any one task
    D. assign the same amount of work to each subordinate

3. Assume that you are a supervisor in charge of a number of   3. ...
workers who do the same kind of work and who each produce
about the same volume of work in a given period of time.
When their performance is evaluated, the worker who should
be rated as the MOST accurate is the one
    A. whose errors are the easiest to correct
    B. whose errors involve the smallest amount of money
    C. who makes the fewest errors in her work
    D. who makes fewer errors as she becomes more experienced

4. As a supervisor, you have been asked by the manager to re-   4. ...
commend whether the work of the bookkeeping office requires
a permanent increase in bookkeeping office staff.
Of the following questions, the one whose answer would be
MOST likely to assist you in making your recommendation is:
    A. Are temporary employees hired to handle seasonal
       fluctuations in work loads?
    B. Are some permanent employees working irregular hours
       because they occasionally work overtime?
    C. Are the present permanent employees keeping the work
       of the bookkeeping office current?
    D. Are employees complaining that the work is unevenly
       divided?

5. Assume that you are a supervisor. One of your subordinates 5. ...
tells you that he is dissatisfied with his work assignment
and that he wishes to discuss the matter with you. The employee is obviously very angry and upset.
Of the following, the course of action that you should take
FIRST in this situation is to
    A. promise the employee that you will review all the work
       assignments in the office to determine whether any
       changes should be made
    B. have the employee present his complaint, correcting
       him whenever he makes what seems to be an erroneous
       charge against you
    C. postpone discussion of the employee's complaint, ex-
       plaining to him that the matter can be settled more
       satisfactorily if it is discussed calmly
    D. permit the employee to present his complaint in full,
       withholding your comments until he has finished making
       his complaint

6. Assume that you are a supervisor. You find that you are   6. ...
spending too much time on routine tasks, and not enough
time on supervision of the work of your subordinates.
It would be *advisable* for you to
    A. assign some of the routine tasks to your subordinates
    B. postpone the performance of routine tasks until you
       have completed your supervisory tasks
    C. delegate the supervisory work to a capable subordinate
    D. eliminate some of the supervisory tasks that you are
       required to perform

7. Assume that you are a supervisor. You discover that one   7. ...
of your workers has violated an important rule.

The FIRST course of action for you as the supervisor to take would be to
- A. call a meeting of the entire staff and discuss the matter generally without mentioning any employee by name
- B. arrange to supervise the offending worker's activities more closely
- C. discuss the violation privately with the worker involved
- D. discuss the matter with the worker within hearing of the entire staff so that she will feel too ashamed to commit this violation in the future

8. As a supervisor, you are to prepare a vacation schedule for the bookkeeping office employees.
The one of the following that is the LEAST important factor for you to consider in setting up this schedule is
- A. seniority
- B. vacation preferences of employees
- C. average producivity of the office
- D. workload

9. In assigning a complicated task to a group of subordinates, a certain supervisor does not indicate the specific steps to be followed in performing the assignment, nor does he designate which subordinate   is to be responsible for seeing that the task is done on time.
This supervisor's method of assigning the task is MOST likely to result in
- A. confusion among subordinates with consequent delays in work
- B. greater individual effort and self-reliance
- C. assumption of authority by capable subordinates
- D. loss of confidence by subordinates in their ability

10. While you are explaining a new procedure to an employee, she asks you a question about the procedure which you cannot answer.
The MOST appropriate action for you to take is to
- A. admit your inability to answer the question and promise to obtain the information
- B. point out the unlikelihood of a situation arising which would require an answer to the question
- C. ask the worker to give her reason for asking the question before you give any further reply
- D. tell her to inform you immediately, should a situation arise requiring an answer to her question

KEYS (CORRECT ANSWERS)

TEST 1				TEST 2				TEST 3				TEST 4	
1.	D	11.	D	1.	D	11.	A	1.	B	11.	B	1.	D
2.	C	12.	A	2.	D	12.	B	2.	A	12.	A	2.	B
3.	B	13.	D	3.	D	13.	C	3.	C	13.	B	3.	C
4.	B	14.	D	4.	A	14.	C	4.	D	14.	B	4.	C
5.	C	15.	D	5.	A	15.	C	5.	A	15.	C	5.	D
6.	D	16.	A	6.	B	16.	B	6.	C	16.	C	6.	A
7.	B	17.	B	7.	D	17.	B	7.	D	17.	D	7.	C
8.	B	18.	B	8.	B	18.	A	8.	A	18.	D	8.	C
9.	A	19.	C	9.	D	19.	D	9.	B	19.	A	9.	A
10.	B	20.	C	10.	D	20.	A	10.	B	20.	B	10.	A
	21.	A			21.	B			21.	B			
	22.	B			22.	C			22.	A			
	23.	B			23.	B			23.	C			
	24.	C			24.	A			24.	A			
	25.	A			25.	B			25.	B			

16

EXAMINATION SECTION
TEST 1

DIRECTIONS: Each question or incomplete statement is followed by several suggested answers or completions. Select the one that BEST answers the question or completes the statement. *PRINT THE LETTER OF THE CORRECT ANSWER IN THE SPACE AT THE RIGHT.*

1. Of the following, the one MOST important quality required   1.___
   of a good supervisor is
   A. ambition   B. leadership
   C. friendliness   D. popularity

2. It is often said that a supervisor can delegate authority   2.___
   but never responsibility.
   This means MOST NEARLY that
   A. a supervisor must do his own work if he expects it to
      be done properly
   B. a supervisor can assign someone else to do his work,
      but in the last analysis, the supervisor himself must
      take the blame for any actions followed
   C. authority and responsibility are two separate things
      that cannot be borne by the same person
   D. it is better for a supervisor never to delegate his
      authority

3. One of your men who is a habitual complainer asks you to   3.___
   grant him a minor privilege.
   Before granting or denying such a request, you should
   consider
   A. the merits of the case
   B. that it is good for group morale to grant a request
      of this nature
   C. the man's seniority
   D. that to deny such a request will lower your standing
      with the men

4. A supervisory practice on the part of a foreman which is   4.___
   MOST likely to lead to confusion and inefficiency is for
   him to
   A. give orders verbally directly to the man assigned to
      the job
   B. issue orders only in writing
   C. follow up his orders after issuing them
   D. relay his orders to the men through co-workers

5. It would be POOR supervision on a foreman's part if he   5.___
   A. asked an experienced maintainer for his opinion on the
      method of doing a special job
   B. make it a policy to avoid criticizing a man in front
      of his co-workers
   C. consulted his assistant supervisor on unusual problems
   D. allowed a cooling-off period of several days before
      giving one of his men a deserved reprimand

6. Of the following behavior characteristics of a supervisor,   6.___
   the one that is MOST likely to lower the morale of the men
   he supervises is
      A. diligence   B. favoritism
      C. punctuality   D. thoroughness

7. Of the following, the BEST method of getting an employee   7.___
   who is not working up to his capacity to produce more work
   is to
      A. have another employee criticize his production
      B. privately criticize his production but encourage him
         to produce more
      C. criticize his production before his associates
      D. criticize his production and threaten to fire him

8. Of the following, the BEST thing for a supervisor to do   8.___
   when a subordinate has done a very good job is to
      A. tell him to take it easy
      B. praise his work
      C. reduce his workload
      D. say nothing because he may become conceited

9. Your orders to your crew are MOST likely to be followed if   9.___
   you
      A. explain the reasons for these orders
      B. warn that all violators will be punished
      C. promise easy assignments to those who follow these
         orders best
      D. say that they are for the good of the department

10. In order to be a good supervisor, you should   10.___
      A. impress upon your men that you demand perfection in
         their work at all times
      B. avoid being blamed for your crew's mistakes
      C. impress your superior with your ability
      D. see to it that your men get what they are entitled to

11. In giving instructions to a crew, you should   11.___
      A. speak in as loud a tone as possible
      B. speak in a coaxing, persuasive manner
      C. speak quietly, clearly, and courteously
      D. always use the word *please* when giving instructions

12. Of the following factors, the one which is LEAST important   12.___
   in evaluating an employee and his work is his
      A. dependability   B. quantity of work done
      C. quality of work done   D. education and training

13. When a District Superintendent first assumes his command,   13.___
   it is LEAST important for him at the beginning to observe
      A. how his equipment is designed and its adaptability
      B. how to reorganize the district for greater efficiency
      C. the capabilities of the men in the district
      D. the methods of operation being employed

14. When making an inspection of one of the buildings under   14.___
    your supervision, the BEST procedure to follow in making
    a record of the inspection is to
      A. return immediately to the office and write a report
         from memory
      B. write down all the important facts during or as soon
         as you complete the inspection
      C. fix in your mind all important facts so that you can
         repeat them from memory if necessary
      D. fix in your mind all important facts so that you can
         make out your report at the end of the day

15. Assume that your superior has directed you to make certain   15.___
    changes in your established procedure. After using this
    modified procedure on several occasions, you find that the
    original procedure was distinctly superior and you wish to
    return to it.
    You should
      A. let your superior find this out for himself
      B. simply change back to the original procedure
      C. compile definite data and information to prove your
         case to your superior
      D. persuade one of the more experienced workers to take
         this matter up with your superior

16. An inspector visited a large building under construction.   16.___
    He inspected the soil lines at 9 A.M., water lines at
    10 A.M., fixtures at 11 A.M., and did his office work in
    the afternoon. He followed the same pattern daily for
    weeks.
    This procedure was
      A. *good*; because it was methodical and he did not miss
         anything
      B. *good*; because it gave equal time to all phases of the
         plumbing
      C. *bad*; because not enough time was devoted to fixtures
      D. *bad*; because the tradesmen knew when the inspection
         would occur

17. Assume that one of the foremen in a training course,   17.___
    which you are conducting, proposes a poor solution for a
    maintenance problem.
    Of the following, the BEST course of action for you to
    take is to
      A. accept the solution tentatively and correct it during
         the next class meeting
      B. point out all the defects of this proposed solution
         and wait until somebody thinks of a better solution
      C. try to get the class to reject this proposed solution
         and develop a better solution
      D. let the matter pass since somebody will present a
         better solution as the class work proceeds

18. As a supervisor, you should be seeking ways to improve   18.____
    the efficiency of shop operations by means such as
    changing established work procedures.
    The following are offered as possible actions that you
    should consider in changing established work procedures:
    I. Make changes only when your foremen agree to them
    II. Discuss changes with your supervisor before putting
        them into practice
    III. Standardize any operation which is performed on a
         continuing basis
    IV. Make changes quickly and quietly in order to avoid
        dissent
    V. Secure expert guidance before instituting unfamiliar
       procedures

    Of the following suggested answers, the one that describes
    the actions to be taken to change established work proce-
    dures is
        A. I, IV, and V *only*   B. II, III, and V *only*
        C. III, IV, and V *only*   D. All of the above

19. A supervisor determined that a foreman, without informing   19.____
    his superior, delegated responsibility for checking time
    cards to a member of his gang. The supervisor then called
    the foreman into his office where he reprimanded the
    foreman.
    This action of the supervisor in reprimanding the foreman
    was
        A. *proper*;because the checking of time cards is the
           foreman's responsibility and should not be delegated
        B. *proper*;because the foreman did not ask the supervisor
           for permission to delegate responsibility
        C. *improper*;because the foreman may no longer take the
           initiative in solving future problems
        D. *improper*;because the supervisor is interfering in a
           function which is not his responsibility

20. A capable supervisor should check all operations under   20.____
    his control.
    Of the following, the LEAST important reason for doing
    this is to make sure that
        A. operations are being performed as scheduled
        B. he personally observes all operations at all times
        C. all the operations are still needed
        D. his manpower is being utilized efficiently

21. A supervisor makes it a practice to apply fair and firm   21.____
    discipline in all cases of rule infractions, including
    those of a minor nature.
    This practice should PRIMARILY be considered
        A. *bad*;since applying discipline for minor violations
           is a waste of time
        B. *good*;because not applying discipline for minor infrac-
           tions can lead to a more serious erosion of discipline
        C. *bad*;because employees do not like to be disciplined
           for minor violations of the rules
        D. *good*;because violating any rule can cause a dangerous
           situation to occur

22. A maintainer would PROPERLY consider it poor supervisory practice for a foreman to consult with him on   22.____
    A. which of several repair jobs should be scheduled first
    B. how to cope with personal problems at home
    C. whether the neatness of his headquarters can be improved
    D. how to express a suggestion which the maintainer plans to submit formally

23. Assume that you have determined that the work of one of your foremen and the men he supervises is consistently behind schedule. When you discuss this situation with the foreman, he tells you that his men are poor workers and then complains that he must spend all of his time checking on their work.   23.____
    The following actions are offered for your consideration as possible ways of solving the problem of poor performance of the foreman and his men:
      I. Review the work standards with the foreman and determine whether they are realistic
     II. Tell the foreman that you will recommend him for the foreman's training course for retraining
    III. Ask the foreman for the names of the maintainers and then replace them as soon as possible
     IV. Tell the foreman that you expect him to meet a satisfactory level of performance
      V. Tell the foreman to insist that his men work overtime to catch up to the schedule
     VI. Tell the foreman to review the type and amount of training he has given the maintainers
    VII. Tell the foreman that he will be out of a job if he does not produce on schedule
   VIII. Avoid all criticism of the foreman and his methods

    Which of the following suggested answers CORRECTLY lists the proper actions to be taken to solve the problem of poor performance of the foreman and his men?
    A. I, II, IV, and VI *only*
    B. I, III, V, and VII *only*
    C. II, III, VI, and VIII *only*
    D. IV, V, VI, and VIII *only*

24. When a conference or a group discussion is tending to turn into a *bull session* without constructive purpose, the BEST action to take is to   24.____
    A. reprimand the leader of the *bull session*
    B. redirect the discussion to the business at hand
    C. dismiss the meeting and reschedule it for another day
    D. allow the *bull session* to continue

25. Assume that you have been assigned responsibility for a program in which a high production rate is mandatory. From past experience, you know that your foremen do not perform equally well in the various types of jobs given to them.   25.____

Which of the following methods should you use in selecting
foremen for the specific types of work involved in the
program?
  A. Leave the method of selecting foremen to your super-
     visor
  B. Assign each foreman to the work he does best
  C. Allow each foreman to choose his own job
  D. Assign each foreman to a job which will permit him
     to improve his own abilities

KEY (CORRECT ANSWERS)

1. B		11. C	
2. B		12. D	
3. A		13. B	
4. D		14. B	
5. D		15. C	
6. B		16. D	
7. B		17. C	
8. B		18. B	
9. A		19. A	
10. D		20. B	

21. B
22. A
23. A
24. B
25. B

TEST 2

DIRECTIONS: Each question or incomplete statement is followed by several suggested answers or completions. Select the one that BEST answers the question or completes the statement. *PRINT THE LETTER OF THE CORRECT ANSWER IN THE SPACE AT THE RIGHT.*

1. A foreman who is familiar with modern management principles should know that the one of the following requirements of an administrator which is LEAST important is his ability to
   A. coordinate work
   B. plan, organize, and direct the work under his control
   C. cooperate with others
   D. perform the duties of the employees under his juris-diction

1.___

2. When subordinates request his advice in solving problems encountered in their work, a certain chief occasionally answers the request by first asking the subordinate what he thinks should be done.
   This action by the chief is, on the whole,
   A. *desirable* because it stimulates subordinates to give more thought to the solution of problems encountered
   B. *undesirable* because it discourages subordinates from asking questions
   C. *desirable* because it discourages subordinates from asking questions
   D. *undesirable* because it undermines the confidence of subordinates in the ability of their supervisor

2.___

3. Of the following factors that may be considered by a unit head in dealing with the tardy subordinate, the one which should be given LEAST consideration is the
   A. frequency with which the employee is tardy
   B. effect of the employee's tardiness upon the work of other employees
   C. willingness of the employee to work overtime when necessary
   D. cause of the employee's tardiness

3.___

4. The MOST important requirement of a good inspectional report is that it should be
   A. properly addressed   B. lengthy
   C. clear and brief   D. spelled correctly

4.___

5. Building superintendents frequently inquire about depart-mental inspectional procedures.
   Of the following, it is BEST to
   A. advise them to write to the department for an official reply
   B. refuse as the inspectional procedure is a restricted matter
   C. briefly explain the procedure to them
   D. avoid the inquiry by changing the subject

5.___

6. Reprimanding a crew member before other workers is a   6.___
   A. *good practice*; the reprimand serves as a warning to
      the other workers
   B. *bad practice*; people usually resent criticism made
      in public
   C. *good practice*; the other workers will realize that
      the supervisor is fair
   D. *bad practice*; the other workers will take sides in
      the dispute

7. Of the following actions, the one which is LEAST likely to   7.___
   promote good work is for the group leader to
   A. praise workers for doing a good job
   B. call attention to the opportunities for promotion for
      better workers
   C. threaten to recommend discharge of workers who are
      below standard
   D. put into practice any good suggestion made by crew
      members

8. A supervisor notices that a member of his crew has skipped   8.___
   a routine step in his job.
   Of the following, the BEST action for the supervisor to
   take is to
   A. promptly question the worker about the incident
   B. immediately assign another man to complete the job
   C. bring up the incident the next time the worker asks
      for a favor
   D. say nothing about the incident but watch the worker
      carefully in the future

9. Assume you have been told to show a new worker how to   9.___
   operate a piece of equipment.
   Your FIRST step should be to
   A. ask the worker if he has any questions about the
      equipment
   B. permit the worker to operate the equipment himself
      while you carefully watch to prevent damage
   C. demonstrate the operation of the equipment for the
      worker
   D. have the worker read an instruction booklet on the
      maintenance of the equipment

10. Whenever a new man was assigned to his crew, the super-   10.___
    visor would introduce him to all other crew members, take
    him on a tour of the plant, tell him about bus schedules
    and places to eat.
    This practice is
    A. *good*; the new man is made to feel welcome
    B. *bad*; supervisors should not interfere in personal
       matters
    C. *good*; the new man knows that he can bring his personal
       problems to the supervisor
    D. *bad*; work time should not be spent on personal matters

11. The MOST important factor in successful leadership is   11.___
    the ability to
    A. obtain instant obedience to all orders
    B. establish friendly personal relations with crew members
    C. avoid disciplining crew members
    D. make crew members want to do what should be done

12. Explaining the reasons for departmental procedure to   12.___
    workers tends to
    A. waste time which should be used for productive purposes
    B. increase their interest in their work
    C. make them more critical of departmental procedures
    D. confuse them

13. If you want a job done well, do it yourself.   13.___
    For a supervisor to follow this advice would be
    A. *good*; a supervisor is responsible for the work of his
       crew
    B. *bad*; a supervisor should train his men, not do their
       work
    C. *good*; a supervisor should be skilled in all jobs
       assigned to his crew
    D. *bad*; a supervisor loses respect when he works with his
       hands

14. When a supervisor discovers a mistake in one of the jobs   14.___
    for which his crew is responsible, it is MOST important
    for him to find out
    A. whether anybody else knows about the mistake
    B. who was to blame for the mistake
    C. how to prevent similar mistakes in the future
    D. whether similar mistakes occurred in the past

15. A supervisor who has to explain a new procedure to his   15.___
    crew should realize that questions from the crew USUALLY
    show that they
    A. are opposed to the new procedure
    B. are completely confused by the explanation
    C. need more training in the new procedure
    D. are interested in the explanation

16. A GOOD way for a supervisor to retain the confidence of   16.___
    his or her employees is to
    A. say as little as possible
    B. check work frequently
    C. make no promises unless they will be fulfilled
    D. never hesitate in giving an answer to any question

17. Good supervision is ESSENTIALLY a matter of   17.___
    A. patience in supervising workers
    B. care in selecting workers
    C. skill in human relations
    D. fairness in disciplining workers

18. It is MOST important for an employee who has been assigned   18.___
    a monotonous task to
    A. perform this task before doing other work
    B. ask another employee to help
    C. perform this task only after all other work has been
       completed
    D. take measures to prevent mistakes in performing the
       task

19. One of your employees has violated a minor agency regula-   19.___
    tion.
    The FIRST thing you should do is
    A. warn the employee that you will have to take disci-
       plinary action if it should happen again
    B. ask the employee to explain his or her actions
    C. inform your supervisor and wait for advice
    D. write a memo describing the incident and place it in
       the employee's personnel file

20. One of your employees tells you that he feels you give   20.___
    him much more work than the other employees, and he is
    having trouble meeting your deadlines.
    You should
    A. ask if he has been under a lot of non-work related
       stress lately
    B. review his recent assignments to determine if he is
       correct
    C. explain that this is a busy time, but you are dividing
       the work equally
    D. tell him that he is the most competent employee and
       that is why he receives more work

21. A supervisor assigns one of his crew to complete a portion   21.___
    of a job. A short time later, the supervisor notices that
    the portion has not been completed.
    Of the following, the BEST way for the supervisor to
    handle this is to
    A. ask the crew member why he has not completed the
       assignment
    B. reprimand the crew member for not obeying orders
    C. assign another crew member to complete the assignment
    D. complete the assignment himself

22. Suppose that a member of your crew complains that you are   22.___
    playing favorites in assigning work.
    Of the following, the BEST method of handling the complaint
    is to
    A. deny it and refuse to discuss the matter with the worker
    B. take the opportunity to tell the worker what is wrong
       with his work
    C. ask the worker for examples to prove his point and try
       to clear up any misunderstanding
    D. promise to be more careful in making assignments in
       the future

23. A member of your crew comes to you with a complaint.   23.___
    After discussing the matter with him, it is clear that
    you have convinced him that his complaint was not justified.
    At this point, you should
    A. permit him to drop the matter
    B. make him admit his error
    C. pretend to see some justification in his complaint
    D. warn him against making unjustified complaints

24. Suppose that a supervisor has in his crew an older man   24.___
    who works rather slowly. In other respects, this man is
    a good worker; he is seldom absent, works carefully, never
    loafs, and is cooperative.
    The BEST way for the supervisor to handle this worker is to
    A. try to get him to work faster and less carefully
    B. give him the most disagreeable job
    C. request that he be given special training
    D. permit him to work at his own speed

25. Suppose that a member of your crew comes to you with a   25.___
    suggestion he thinks will save time in doing a job. You
    realize immediately that it won't work.
    Under these circumstances, your BEST action would be to
    A. thank the worker for the suggestion and forget about it
    B. explain to the worker why you think it won't work
    C. tell the worker to put the suggestion in writing
    D. ask the other members of your crew to criticize the
       suggestion

KEY (CORRECT ANSWERS)

1. D		11. D	
2. A		12. B	
3. C		13. B	
4. C		14. C	
5. C		15. D	
6. B		16. C	
7. C		17. C	
8. A		18. D	
9. C		19. B	
10. A		20. B	

21. A
22. C
23. A
24. D
25. B

PHILOSOPHY, PRINCIPLES, PRACTICES, AND TECHNICS
OF
SUPERVISION, ADMINISTRATION, MANAGEMENT, AND ORGANIZATION

I. MEANING OF SUPERVISION

The extension of the democratic philosophy has been accompanied by an extension in the scope of supervision. Modern leaders and supervisors no longer think of supervision in the narrow sense of being confined chiefly to visiting employees, supplying materials, or rating the staff. They regard supervision as being intimately related to all the concerned agencies of society, they speak of the supervisor's function in terms of "growth", rather than the "improvement," of employees

This modern concept of supervision may be defined as follows:

Supervision is leadership and the development of leadership within groups which are cooperatively engaged in inspection, research, training, guidance and evaluation.

II. THE OLD AND THE NEW SUPERVISION

TRADITIONAL	*MODERN*
1. Inspection	1. Study and analysis
2. Focused on the employee	2. Focused on aims, materials, methods, supervisors, employees, environment
3. Visitation	3. Demonstrations, intervisitation, workshops, directed reading, bulletins, etc.
4. Random and haphazard	4. Definitely organized and planned (scientific)
5. Imposed and authoritarian	5. Cooperative and democratic
6. One person usually	6. Many persons involved (creative)

III. THE EIGHT (8) BASIC PRINCIPLES OF THE NEW SUPERVISION

1. *PRINCIPLE OF RESPONSIBILITY*

Authority to act and responsibility for acting must be joined.
   a. If you give responsibility, give authority.
   b. Define employee duties clearly.
   c. Protect employees from criticism by others.
   d. Recognize the rights as well as obligations of employees.
   e. Achieve the aims of a democratic society insofar as it is possible within the area of your work.
   f. Establish a situation favorable to training and learning.
   g. Accept ultimate responsibility for everything done in your section, unit, office, division, department.
   h. Good administration and good supervision are inseparable.

2. *PRINCIPLE OF AUTHORITY*

The success of the supervisor is measured by the extent to which the power of authority is not used.
   a. Exercise simplicity and informality in supervision.
   b. Use the simplest machinery of supervision.
   c. If it is good for the organization as a whole, it is probably justified.
   d. Seldom be arbitrary or authoritative.
   e. Do not base your work on the power of position or of personality.
   f. Permit and encourage the free expression of opinions.

3. *PRINCIPLE OF SELF-GROWTH*

The success of the supervisor is measured by the extent to which, and the speed with which, he is no longer needed.
   a. Base criticism on principles, not on specifics.
   b. Point out higher activities to employees.

     c. Train for self-thinking by employees,to meet new situations.
     d. Stimulate initiative,self-reliance and individual responsibility.
     e. Concentrate on stimulating the growth of employees rather than
        on removing defects.

4. *PRINCIPLE OF INDIVIDUAL WORTH*
   Respect for the individual is a paramount consideration in supervision.
     a. Be human and sympathetic in dealing with employees.
     b. Don't nag about things to be done.
     c. Recognize the individual differences among employees and seek
        opportunities to permit best expression of each personality.

5. *PRINCIPLE OF CREATIVE LEADERSHIP*
   The best supervision is that which is not apparent to the employee.
     a. Stimulate,don't drive employees to creative action.
     b. Emphasize doing good things.
     c. Encourage employees to do what they do best.
     d. Do not be too greatly concerned with details of subject or
        method.
     e. Do not be concerned exclusively with immediate problems and
        activities.
     f. Reveal higher activities and make them both desired and maxi-
        mally possible.
     g. Determine procedures in the light of each situation but see
        that these are derived from a sound basic philosophy.
     h. Aid, inspire and lead so as to liberate the creative spirit
        latent in all good employees.

6. *PRINCIPLE OF SUCCESS AND FAILURE*
   There are no unsuccessful employees, only unsuccessful supervisors
  who have failed to give proper leadership.
     a. Adapt suggestions to the capacities, attitudes, and prejudices
        of employees.
     b. Be gradual, be progressive, be persistent.
     c. Help the employee find the general principle; have the employee
        apply his own problem to the general principle.
     d. Give adequate appreciation for good work and honest effort.
     e. Anticipate employee difficulties and help to prevent them.
     f. Encourage employees to do the desirable things they will do
        anyway.
     g. Judge your supervision by the results it secures.

7. *PRINCIPLE OF SCIENCE*
   Successful supervision is scientific,objective,and experimental.
  It is based on facts, not on prejudices.
     a. Be cumulative in results.
     b. Never divorce your suggestions from the goals of training.
     c. Don't be impatient of results.
     d. Keep all matters on a professional, not a personal level.
     e. Do not be concerned exclusively with immediate problems and
        activities.
     f. Use objective means of determining achievement and rating.
        where possible.

8. *PRINCIPLE OF COOPERATION*
   Supervision is a cooperative enterprise between supervisor
  and employee.
     a. Begin with conditions as they are.
     b. Ask opinions of all involved when formulating policies.

c. Organization is as good as its weakest link.
d. Let employees help to determine policies and department programs.
e. Be approachable and accessible - physically and mentally.
f. Develop pleasant social relationships.

IV. WHAT IS ADMINISTRATION?

Administration is concerned with providing the environment, the material facilities, and the operational procedures that will promote the maximum growth and development of supervisors and employees. (Organization is an aspect, and a concomitant, of administration.)

There is no sharp line of demarcation between supervision and administration; these functions are intimately interrelated and, often, overlapping. They are complementary activities.

1. *PRACTICES COMMONLY CLASSED AS "SUPERVISORY"*
   a. Conducting employees conferences
   b. Visiting sections, units, offices, divisions, departments
   c. Arranging for demonstrations
   d. Examining plans
   e. Suggesting professional reading
   f. Interpreting bulletins
   g. Recommending in-service training courses
   h. Encouraging experimentation
   i. Appraising employee morale
   j. Providing for intervisitation

2. *PRACTICES COMMONLY CLASSIFIED AS "ADMINISTRATIVE"*
   a. Management of the office
   b. Arrangement of schedules for extra duties
   c. Assignment of rooms or areas
   d. Distribution of supplies
   e. Keeping records and reports
   f. Care of audio-visual materials
   g. Keeping inventory records
   h. Checking record cards and books
   i. Programming special activities
   j. Checking on the attendance and punctuality of employees

3. *PRACTICES COMMONLY CLASSIFIED AS BOTH "SUPERVISORY" AND "ADMINISTRATIVE"*
   a. Program construction
   b. Testing or evaluating outcomes
   c. Personnel accounting
   d. Ordering instructional materials

V. RESPONSIBILITIES OF THE SUPERVISOR

A person employed in a supervisory capacity must constantly be able to improve his own efficiency and ability. He represents the employer to the employees and only continuous self-examination can make him a capable supervisor.

Leadership and training are the supervisor's responsibility. An efficient working unit is one in which the employees work with the supervisor. It is his job to bring out the best in his employees. He must always be relaxed, courteous and calm in his association with his employees. Their feelings are important, and a harsh attitude does not develop the most efficient employees.

3

VI. COMPETENCIES OF THE SUPERVISOR

1. Complete knowledge of the duties and responsibilities of his position.
2. To be able to organize a job, plan ahead and carry through.
3. To have self-confidence and initiative.
4. To be able to handle the unexpected situation and make quick decisions.
5. To be able to properly train subordinates in the positions they are best suited for.
6. To be able to keep good human relations among his subordinates.
7. To be able to keep good human relations between his subordinates and himself and to earn their respect and trust.

VII. THE PROFESSIONAL SUPERVISOR-EMPLOYEE RELATIONSHIP

There are two kinds of efficiency: one kind is only apparent and is produced in organizations through the exercise of mere discipline; this is but a simulation of the second, or true, efficiency which springs from spontaneous cooperation. If you are a manager, no matter how great or small your responsibility, it is your job, in the final analysis, to create and develop this involuntary cooperation among the people whom you supervise. For, no matter how powerful a combination of money, machines, and materials a company may have, this is a dead and sterile thing without a team of willing, thinking and articulate people to guide it.

The following 21 points are presented as indicative of the exemplary basic relationship that should exist between supervisor and employee:

1. Each person wants to be liked and respected by his fellow employee and wants to be treated with consideration and respect by his superior.
2. The most competent employee will make an error. However, in a unit where good relations exist between the supervisor and his employees, tenseness and fear do not exist. Thus, errors are not hidden or covered up and the efficiency of a unit is not impaired.
3. Subordinates resent rules, regulations, or orders that are unreasonable or unexplained.
4. Subordinates are quick to resent unfairness, harshness, injustices and favoritism.
5. An employee will accept responsibility if he knows that he will be complimented for a job well done, and not too harshly chastized for failure; that his supervisor will check the cause of the failure, and, if it was the supervisor's fault, he will assume the blame therefor. If it was the employee's fault, his supervisor will explain the correct method or means of handling the responsibility.
6. An employee wants to receive credit for a suggestion he has made, that is used. If a suggestion cannot be used, the employee is entitled to an explanation. The supervisor should not say "no" and close the subject.
7. Fear and worry slow up a worker's ability. Poor working environment can impair his physical and mental health. A good supervisor avoids forceful methods, threats and arguments to get a job done.
8. A forceful supervisor is able to train his employees individually and as a team, and is able to motivate them in the proper channels.

4

9. A mature supervisor is able to properly evaluate his subordinates and to keep them happy and satisfied.
10. A sensitive supervisor will never patronize his subordinates.
11. A worthy supervisor will respect his employees' confidences.
12. Definite and clear-cut responsibilities should be assigned to each executive.
13. Responsibility should always be coupled with corresponding authority.
14. No change should be made in the scope or responsibilities of a position without a definite understanding to that effect on the part of all persons concerned.
15. No executive or employee, occupying a single position in the organization, should be subject to definite orders from more than one source.
16. Orders should never be given to subordinates over the head of a responsible executive. Rather than do this, the officer in question should be supplanted.
17. Criticisms of subordinates should, whever possible, be made privately, and in no case should a subordinate be criticized in the presence of executives or employees of equal or lower rank.
18. No dispute or difference between executives or employees as to authority or responsibilities should be considered too trivial for prompt and careful adjudication.
19. Promotions, wage changes, and disciplinary action should always be approved by the executive immediately superior to the one directly responsible.
20. No executive or employee should ever be required, or expected, to be at the same time an assistant to, and critic of, another.
21. Any executive whose work is subject to regular inspection should, whever practicable, be given the assistance and facilities necessary to enable him to maintain an independent check of the quality of his work.

VIII. MINI-TEXT IN SUPERVISION, ADMINISTRATION, MANAGEMENT, AND ORGANIZATION
A. BRIEF HIGHLIGHTS
Listed concisely and sequentially are major headings and important data in the field for quick recall and review.
1. *LEVELS OF MANAGEMENT*
Any organization of some size has several levels of management. In terms of a ladder the levels are:

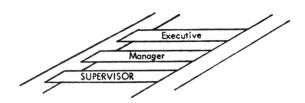

The first level is very important because it is the beginning point of management leadership.
2. *WHAT THE SUPERVISOR MUST LEARN*
A supervisor must learn to:
(1) Deal with people and their differences
(2) Get the job done through people
(3) Recognize the problems when they exist
(4) Overcome obstacles to good performance
(5) Evaluate the performance of people
(6) Check his own performance in terms of accomplishment

3. *A DEFINITION OF SUPERVISOR*
    The term supervisor means any individual having authority, in the interests of the employer, to hire, transfer, suspend, lay-off, recall, promote, discharge, assign, reward, or discipline other employees... or responsibility to direct them, or to adjust their grievances, or effectively to recommend such action, if, in connection with the foregoing, exercise of such authority is not of a merely routine or clerical nature but requires the use of independent judgment.

4. *ELEMENTS OF THE TEAM CONCEPT*
    What is involved in teamwork? The component parts are:
    (1) Members   (3) Goals   (5) Cooperation
    (2) A leader   (4) Plans   (6) Spirit

5. *PRINCIPLES OF ORGANIZATION*
    (1) A team member must know what his job is
    (2) Be sure that the nature and scope of a job are understood
    (3) Authority and responsibility should be carefully spelled out
    (4) A supervisor should be permitted to make the maximum number of decisions affecting his employees
    (5) Employees should report to only one supervisor
    (6) A supervisor should direct only as many employees as he can handle effectively
    (7) An organization plan should be flexible
    (8) Inspection and performance of work should be separate
    (9) Organizational problems should receive immediate attention
    (10) Assign work in line with ability and experience

6. *THE FOUR IMPORTANT PARTS OF EVERY JOB*
    (1) Inherent in every job is the *accountability* for results
    (2) A second set of factors in every job are *responsibilities*
    (3) Along with duties and responsibilities one must have the *authority* to act within certain limits without obtaining permission to proceed
    (4) No job exists in a vacuum. The supervisor is surrounded by key *relationships*

7. *PRINCIPLES OF DELEGATION*
    Where work is delegated for the first time, the supervisor should think in terms of these questions:
    (1) Who is best qualified to do this?
    (2) Can an employee improve his abilities by doing this?
    (3) How long should an employee spend on this?
    (4) Are there any special problems for which he will need guidance?
    (5) How broad a delegation can I make?

8. *PRINCIPLES OF EFFECTIVE COMMUNICATIONS*
    (1) Determine the media
    (2) To whom directed?
    (3) Identification and source authority
    (4) Is communication understood?

9. *PRINCIPLES OF WORK IMPROVEMENT*
    (1) Most people usually do only the work which is assigned to them
    (2) Workers are likely to fit assigned work into the time available to perform it
    (3) A good workload usually stimulates output
    (4) People usually do their best work when they know that results will be reviewed or inspected

(5) Employees usually feel that someone else is responsible for conditions of work, workplace layout, job methods, type of tools and equipment, and other such factors

(6) Employees are usually defensive about their job security

(7) Employees have natural resistance to change

(8) Employees can support or destroy a supervisor

(9) A supervisor usually earns the respect of his people through his personal example of diligence and efficiency

10. *AREAS OF JOB IMPROVEMENT*

The *areas* of job improvement are quite numerous, but the most common ones which a supervisor can identify and utilize are:

(1) Departmental layout
(2) Flow of work
(3) Workplace layout
(4) Utilization of manpower
(5) Work methods
(6) Materials handling
(7) Utilization
(8) Motion economy

11. *SEVEN KEY POINTS IN MAKING IMPROVEMENTS*

(1) Select the job to be improved
(2) Study how it is being done now
(3) Question the present method
(4) Determine actions to be taken
(5) Chart proposed method
(6) Get approval and apply
(7) Solicit worker participation

12. *CORRECTIVE TECHNIQUES OF JOB IMPROVEMENT*

Specific Problems	*General Problems*	*Corrective Technique*
(1) Size of workload	(1) Departmental layout	(1) Study with scale model
(2) Inability to meet schedules	(2) Flow of work	(2) Flow chart study
(3) Strain and fatigue	(3) Workplan layout	(3) Motion analysis
(4) Improper use of men and skills	(4) Utilization of manpower	(4) Comparison of units produced to standard allowances
(5) Waste, poor quality, unsafe conditions	(5) Work methods	(5) Methods analysis
(6) Bottleneck conditions that hinder output	(6) Materials handling	(6) Flow chart and equipment study
(7) Poor utilization of equipment and machines	(7) Utilization of equipment	(7) Down time vs. running time
(8) Efficiency and productivity of labor	(8) Motion economy	(8) Motion analysis

13. *A PLANNING CHECKLIST*

(1) Objectives
(2) Controls
(3) Delegations
(4) Communications
(5) Resources
(6) Methods and procedures
(7) Manpower
(8) Equipment
(9) Supplies and materials
(10) Utilization of time
(11) Safety
(12) Money
(13) Work
(14) Timing of improvements

14. *FIVE CHARACTERISTICS OF GOOD DIRECTIONS*

In order to get results, directions must be:

(1) Possible of accomplishment
(2) Agreeable with worker interests
(3) Related to mission
(4) Planned and complete
(5) Unmistakably clear

15. *TYPES OF DIRECTIONS*
        (1) Demands or direct orders   (3) Suggestion or implication
        (2) Requests   (4) Volunteering

16. *CONTROLS*
    A typical listing of the overall areas in which the supervisor should establish controls might be:

(1) Manpower	(4) Quantity of work	(7) Money
(2) Materials	(5) Time	(8) Methods
(3) Quality of work	(6) Space	

17. *ORIENTING THE NEW EMPLOYEE*
        (1) Prepare for him   (3) Orientation for the job
        (2) Welcome the new employee (4) Follow-up

18. *CHECKLIST FOR ORIENTING NEW EMPLOYEES*

                                                  Yes No

(1) Do your appreciate the feelings of new employees when they first report for work? ... ...

(2) Are you aware of the fact that the new employee
must make a big adjustment to his job? ... ...

(3) Have you given him good reasons for liking the
job and the organization? ... ...

(4) Have you prepared for his first day on the job? ... ...

(5) Did you welcome him cordially and make him feel
needed? ... ...

(6) Did you establish rapport with him so that he
feels free to talk and discuss matters with you?... ...

(7) Did you explain his job to him and his relationship to you? ... ...

(8) Does he know that his work will be evaluated periodically on a basis that is fair and objective?.. ...

(9) Did you introduce him to his fellow workers in
such a way that they are likely to accept him? ... ...

(10) Does he know what employee benefits he will receive? ... ...

(11) Does he understand the importance of being on
the job and what to do if he must leave his
duty station? ... ...

(12) Has he been impressed with the importance of accident prevention and safe practice? ... ...

(13) Does he generally know his way around the department? ... ...

(14) Is he under the guidance of a sponsor who will
teach the right ways of doing things? ... ...

(15) Do you plan to follow-up so that he will continue to adjust successfully to his job? ... ...

19. *PRINCIPLES OF LEARNING*
        (1) Motivation (2) Demonstration or explanation
        (3) Practice

20. *CAUSES OF POOR PERFORMANCE*

(1) Improper training for job	(6) Lack of standards of
(2) Wrong tools	performance
(3) Inadequate directions	(7) Wrong work habits
(4) Lack of supervisory follow-up	(8) Low morale
(5) Poor communications	(9) Other

21. *FOUR MAJOR STEPS IN ON-THE-JOB INSTRUCTION*
        (1) Prepare the worker   (3) Tryout performance
        (2) Present the operation   (4) Follow-up

22. *EMPLOYEES WANT FIVE THINGS*
      (1) Security   (2) Opportunity (3) Recognition
      (4) Inclusion (5) Expression

23. *SOME DON'TS IN REGARD TO PRAISE*
      (1) Don't praise a person for something he hasn't done
      (2) Don't praise a person unless you can be sincere
      (3) Don't be sparing in praise just because your superior
           withholds it from you
      (4) Don't let too much time elapse between good performance
           and recognition of it

24. *HOW TO GAIN YOUR WORKERS' CONFIDENCE*
    Methods of developing confidence include such things as:
      (1) Knowing the interests, habits, hobbies of employees
      (2) Admitting your own inadequacies
      (3) Sharing and telling of confidence in others
      (4) Supporting people when they are in trouble
      (5) Delegating matters that can be well handled
      (6) Being frank and straightforward about problems and work-
           ing conditions
      (7) Encouraging others to bring their problems to you
      (8) Taking action on problems which impede worker progress

25. *SOURCES OF EMPLOYEE PROBLEMS*
    On-the-job causes might be such things as:
      (1) A feeling that favoritism is exercised in assignments
      (2) Assignment of overtime
      (3) An undue amount of supervision
      (4) Changing methods or systems
      (5) Stealing of ideas or trade secrets
      (6) Lack of interest in job
      (7) Threat of reduction in force
      (8) Ignorance or lack of communications
      (9) Poor equipment
    (10) Lack of knowing how supervisor feels toward employee
    (11) Shift assignments
    Off-the-job problems might have to do with:
      (1) Health (2) Finances (3) Housing (4) Family

26. *THE SUPERVISOR'S KEY TO DISCIPLINE*
    There are several key points about discipline which the super-
    visor should keep in mind:
      (1) Job discipline is one of the disciplines of life and is
           directed by the supervisor.
      (2) It is more important to correct an employee fault than to
           fix blame for it.
      (3) Employee performance is affected by problems both on the
           job and off.
      (4) Sudden or abrupt changes in behavior can be indications of
           important employee problems.
      (5) Problems should be dealt with as soon as possible after
           they are identified.
      (6) The attitude of the supervisor may have more to do with
           solving problems than the techniques of problem solving.
      (7) Correction of employee behavior should be resorted to only
           after the supervisor is sure that training or counseling
           will not be helpful
      (8) Be sure to document your disciplinary actions.

(9) Make sure that you are disciplining on the basis of facts rather than personal feelings.

(10) Take each disciplinary step in order, being careful not to make snap judgments, or decisions based on impatience.

27. *FIVE IMPORTANT PROCESSES OF MANAGEMENT*
  (1) Planning   (2) Organizing   (3) Scheduling
  (4) Controlling   (5) Motivating

28. *WHEN THE SUPERVISOR FAILS TO PLAN*
  (1) Supervisor creates impression of not knowing his job
  (2) May lead to excessive overtime
  (3) Job runs itself-- supervisor lacks control
  (4) Deadlines and appointments missed
  (5) Parts of the work go undone
  (6) Work interrupted by emergencies
  (7) Sets a bad example
  (8) Uneven workload creates peaks and valleys
  (9) Too much time on minor details at expense of more important tasks

29. *FOURTEEN GENERAL PRINCIPLES OF MANAGEMENT*
  (1) Division of work
  (2) Authority and responsibility
  (3) Discipline
  (4) Unity of command
  (5) Unity of direction
  (6) Subordination of individual interest to general interest
  (7) Remuneration of personnel
  (8) Centralization
  (9) Scalar chain
  (10) Order
  (11) Equity
  (12) Stability of tenure of personnel
  (13) Initiative
  (14) Esprit de corps

30. *CHANGE*

Bringing about change is perhaps attempted more often, and yet less well understood, than anything else the supervisor does. How do people generally react to change? (People tend to resist change that is imposed upon them by other individuals or circumstances.)

Change is characteristic of every situation. It is a part of **every** real endeavor where the efforts of people are concerned.

  A. Why do people resist change?
    People may resist change because of:
    (1) Fear of the unknown
    (2) Implied criticism
    (3) Unpleasant experiences in the past
    (4) Fear of loss of status
    (5) Threat to the ego
    (6) Fear of loss of economic stability
  B. How can we best overcome the resistance to change?
    In initiating change, take these steps:
    (1) Get ready to sell
    (2) identify sources of help
    (3) Anticipate objections
    (4) Sell benefits
    (5) Listen in depth
    (6) Follow up

I. WHO/WHAT IS THE SUPERVISOR?

1. The supervisor is often called the "highest level employee and the lowest level manager."
2. A supervisor is a member of both management and the work group. He acts as a bridge between the two.
3. Most problems in supervision are in the area of human relations, or people problems.
4. Employees expect: Respect, opportunity to learn and to advance, and a sense of belonging, and so forth.
5. Supervisors are responsible for directing people and organizing work. Planning is of paramount importance.
6. A position description is a set of duties and responsibilities inherent to a given position.
7. It is important to keep the position description up-to-date and to provide each employee with his own copy.

II. THE SOCIOLOGY OF WORK

1. People are alike in many ways; however each individual is unique.
2. The supervisor is challenged in getting to know employee differences. Acquiring skills in evaluating individuals is an asset.
3. Maintaining meaningful working relationships in the organization is of great importance.
4. The supervisor has an obligation to help individuals to develop to their fullest potential.
5. Job rotation on a planned basis helps to build versatility and to maintain interest and enthusiasm in work groups.
6. Cross training (job rotation) provides backup skills.
7. The supervisor can help reduce tension by maintaining a sense of humor, providing guidance to employees, and by making reasonable and timely decisions. Employees respond favorably to working under reasonably predictable circumstances.
8. Change is characteristic of all managerial behavior. The supervisor must adjust to changes in procedures, new methods, technological changes, and to a number of new and sometimes challenging situations.
9. To overcome the natural tendency for people to resist change, the supervisor should become more skillful in initiating change.

III. PRINCIPLES AND PRACTICES OF SUPERVISION

1. Employees should be required to answer to only one superior.
2. A supervisor can effectively direct only a limited number of employees, depending upon the complexity, variety, and proximity of the jobs involved.
3. The organizational chart presents the organization in graphic form. It reflects lines of authority and responsibility as well as interrelationships of units within the organization.
4. Distribution of work can be improved through an analysis using the "Work Distribution Chart."
5. The "Work Distribution Chart" reflects the division of work within a unit in understandable form.
6. When related tasks are given to an employee, he has a better chance of increasing his skills through training.
7. The individual who is given the responsibility for tasks must also be given the appropriate authority to insure adequate results.
8. The supervisor should delegate repetitive, routine work. Preparation of recurring reports, maintaining leave and attendance records are some examples.

9. Good discipline is essential to good task performance. Discipline is reflected in the actions of employees on the job in the absence of supervision.
10. Disciplinary action may have to be taken when the positive aspects of discipline have failed. Reprimand, warning, and suspension are examples of disciplinary action.
11. If a situation calls for a reprimand, be sure it is deserved and remember it is to be done in private.

IV. DYNAMIC LEADERSHIP
1. A style is a personal method or manner of exerting influence.
2. Authoritarian leaders often see themselves as the source of power and authority.
3. The democratic leader often perceives the group as the source of authority and power.
4. Supervisors tend to do better when using the pattern of leadership that is most natural for them.
5. Social scientists suggest that the effective supervisor use the leadership style that best fits the problem or circumstances involved.
6. All four styles -- telling, selling, consulting, joining -- have their place. Using one does not preclude using the other at another time.
7. The theory X point of view assumes that the average person dislikes work, will avoid it whenever possible, and must be coerced to achieve organizational objectives.
8. The theory Y point of view assumes that the average person considers work to be as natural as play, and, when the individual is committed, he requires little supervision or direction to accomplish desired objectives.
9. The leader's basic assumptions concerning human behavior and human nature affect his actions, decisions, and other managerial practices.
10. Dissatisfaction among employees is often present, but difficult to isolate. The supervisor should seek to weaken dissatisfaction by keeping promises, being sincere and considerate, keeping employees informed, and so forth.
11. Constructive suggestions should be encouraged during the natural progress of the work.

V. PROCESSES FOR SOLVING PROBLEMS
1. People find their daily tasks more meaningful and satisfying when they can improve them.
2. The causes of problems, or the key factors, are often hidden in the background. Ability to solve problems often involves the ability to isolate them from their backgrounds. There is some substance to the cliché that some persons "can't see the forest for the trees."
3. New procedures are often developed from old ones. Problems should be broken down into manageable parts. New ideas can be adapted from old ones.
4. People think differently in problem-solving situations. Using a logical, patterned approach is often useful. One approach found to be useful includes these steps:
   (a) Define the problem   (d) Weigh and decide
   (b) Establish objectives   (e) Take action
   (c) Get the facts   (f) Evaluate action

VI. TRAINING FOR RESULTS

1. Participants respond best when they feel training is important to them.
2. The supervisor has responsibility for the training and development of those who report to him.
3. When training is delegated to others, great care must be exercised to insure the trainer has knowledge, aptitude, and interest for his work as a trainer.
4. Training (learning) of some type goes on continually. The most successful supervisor makes certain the learning contributes in a productive manner to operational goals.
5. New employees are particularly susceptible to training. Older employees facing new job situations require specific training, as well as having need for development and growth opportunities.
6. Training needs require continuous monitoring.
7. The training officer of an agency is a professional with a responsibility to assist supervisors in solving training problems.
8. Many of the self-development steps important to the supervisor's own growth are equally important to the development of peers and subordinates. Knowledge of these is important when the supervisor consults with others on development and growth opportunities.

VII. HEALTH, SAFETY, AND ACCIDENT PREVENTION

1. Management-minded supervisors take appropriate measures to assist employees in maintaining health and in assuring safe practices in the work environment.
2. Effective safety training and practices help to avoid injury and accidents.
3. Safety should be a management goal. All infractions of safety which are observed should be corrected without exception.
4. Employees' safety attitude, training and instruction, provision of safe tools and equipment, supervision, and leadership are considered highly important factors which contribute to safety and which can be influenced directly by supervisors.
5. When accidents do occur they should be investigated promptly for very important reasons, including the fact that information which is gained can be used to prevent accidents in the future.

VIII. EQUAL EMPLOYMENT OPPORTUNITY

1. The supervisor should endeavor to treat all employees fairly, without regard to religion, race, sex, or national origin.
2. Groups tend to reflect the attitude of the leader. Prejudice can be detected even in very subtle form. Supervisors must strive to create a feeling of mutual respect and confidence in every employee.
3. Complete utilization of all human resources is a national goal. Equitable consideration should be accorded women in the work force, minority-group members, the physically and mentally handicapped, and the older employee. The important question is: "Who can do the job?"
4. Training opportunities, recognition for performance, overtime assignments, promotional opportunities, and all other personnel actions are to be handled on an equitable basis.

IX. IMPROVING COMMUNICATIONS

1. Communications is achieving understanding between the sender and the receiver of a message. It also means sharing information -- the creation of understanding.
2. Communication is basic to all human activity. Words are means of conveying meanings; however, real meanings are in people.
3. There are very practical differences in the effectiveness of one-way, impersonal, and two-way communications. Words spoken face-to-face are better understood. Telephone conversations are effective, but lack the rapport of person-to-person exchanges. The whole person communicates.
4. Cooperation and communication in an organization go hand-in-hand. When there is a mutual respect between people, spelling out rules and procedures for communicating is unnecessary.
5. There are several barriers to effective communications. These include failure to listen with respect and understanding, lack of skill in feedback, and misinterpreting the meanings of words used by the speaker. It is also common practice to listen to what we want to hear, and tune out things we do not want to hear.
6. Communication is management's chief problem. The supervisor should accept the challenge to communicate more effectively and to improve interagency and intra-agency communications.
7. The supervisor may often plan for and conduct meetings. The planning phase is critical and may determine the success or the failure of a meeting.
8. Speaking before groups usually requires extra effort. Stage fright may never disappear completely, but it can be controlled.

X. SELF-DEVELOPMENT

1. Every employee is responsible for his own self-development.
2. Toastmaster and toastmistress clubs offer opportunities to improve skills in oral communications.
3. Planning for one's own self-development is of vital importance. Supervisors know their own strengths and limitations better than anyone else.
4. Many opportunities are open to aid the supervisor in his developmental efforts, including job assignments; training opportunities, both governmental and non-governmental -- to include universities and professional conferences and seminars.
5. Programmed instruction offers a means of studying at one's own rate.
6. Where difficulties may arise from a supervisor's being away from his work for training, he may participate in televised home study or correspondence courses to meet his self-development needs.

XI. TEACHING AND TRAINING

A. The Teaching Process

Teaching is encouraging and guiding the learning activities of students toward established goals. In most cases this process consists in five steps: preparation, presentation, summarization, evaluation, and application.

1. Preparation

   Preparation is twofold in nature; that of the supervisor and the employee.

   Preparation by the supervisor is absolutely essential to success. He must know what, when, where, how, and whom he will teach. Some of the factors that should be considered are:

   (1) The objectives (5) Employee interest
   (2) The materials needed (6) Training aids
   (3) The methods to be used (7) Evaluation
   (4) Employee participation (8) Summarization

   Employee preparation consists in preparing the employee to receive the material. Probably the most important single factor in the preparation of the employee is arousing and maintaining his interest. He must know the objectives of the training, why he is there, how the material can be used, and its importance to him.

2. Presentation

   In presentation, have a carefully designed plan and follow it. The plan should be accurate and complete, yet flexible enough to meet situations as they arise. The method of presentation will be determined by the particular situation and objectives.

3. Summary

   A summary should be made at the end of every training unit and program. In addition, there may be internal summaries depending on the nature of the material being taught. The important thing is that the trainee must always be able to understand how each part of the new material relates to the whole.

4. Application

   The supervisor must arrange work so the employee will be given a chance to apply new knowledge or skills while the material is still clear in his mind and interest is high. The trainee does not really know whether he has learned the material until he has been given a chance to apply it. If the material is not applied, it loses most of its value.

5. Evaluation

   The purpose of all training is to promote learning. To determine whether the training has been a success or failure, the supervisor must evaluate this learning.

   In the broadest sense evaluation includes all the devices, methods, skills, and techniques used by the supervisor to keep himself and the employees informed as to their progress toward the objectives they are pursuing. The extent to which the employee has mastered the knowledge, skills, and abilities, or changed his attitudes, as determined by the program objectives, is the extent to which instruction has succeeded or failed.

   Evaluation should not be confined to the end of the lesson, day, or program but should be used continuously. We shall note later the way this relates to the rest of the teaching process.

B. Teaching Methods

   A teaching method is a pattern of identifiable student and instructor activity used in presenting training material.

   All supervisors are faced with the problem of deciding which method should be used at a given time.

1. Lecture
      The lecture is direct oral presentation of material by the
   supervisor. The present trend is to place less emphasis on the
   trainer's activity and more on that of the trainee.
2. Discussion
      Teaching by discussion or conference involves using questions
   and other techniques to arouse interest and focus attention upon
   certain areas, and by doing so creating a learning situation.
   This can be one of the most valuable methods because it gives
   the employees an opportunity to express their ideas and pool
   their knowledge.
3. Demonstration
      The demonstration is used to teach how something works or how
   to do something. It can be used to show a principle or what the
   results of a series of actions will be. A well-staged demonstration is particularly effective because it shows proper methods
   of performance in a realistic manner.
4. Performance
      Performance is one of the most fundamental of all learning
   techniques or teaching methods. The trainee may be able to tell
   how a specific operation should be performed but he cannot be
   sure he knows how to perform the operation until he has done so.

   As with all methods, there are certain advantages and disadvantages
to each method.

5. Which Method to Use
      Moreover, there are other methods and techniques of teaching.
   It is difficult to use any method without other methods entering into it. In any learning situation a combination of methods
   is usually more effective than any one method alone.

   Finally, evaluation must be integrated into the other aspects of the
teaching-learning process.
   It must be used in the motivation of the trainees; it must be used
to assist in developing understanding during the training; and it must
be related to employee application of the results of training.
   This is distinctly the role of the supervisor.

———

ANSWER SHEET

TEST NO. _____ PART _____ TITLE OF POSITION _____

(AS GIVEN IN EXAMINATION ANNOUNCEMENT - INCLUDE OPTION, IF ANY)

PLACE OF EXAMINATION _____ DATE _____

(CITY OR TOWN)   (STATE)

RATING

USE THE SPECIAL PENCIL.   MAKE GLOSSY BLACK MARKS.

	A	B	C	D	E		A	B	C	D	E		A	B	C	D	E		A	B	C	D	E		A	B	C	D	E
1						26						51						76						101					
2						27						52						77						102					
3						28						53						78						103					
4						29						54						79						104					
5						30						55						80						105					
6						31						56						81						106					
7						32						57						82						107					
8						33						58						83						108					
9						34						59						84						109					
10						35						60						85						110					

Make only ONE mark for each answer.   Additional and stray marks may be
counted as mistakes.   In making corrections, erase errors COMPLETELY.

	A	B	C	D	E		A	B	C	D	E		A	B	C	D	E		A	B	C	D	E		A	B	C	D	E
11						36						61						86						111					
12						37						62						87						112					
13						38						63						88						113					
14						39						64						89						114					
15						40						65						90						115					
16						41						66						91						116					
17						42						67						92						117					
18						43						68						93						118					
19						44						69						94						119					
20						45						70						95						120					
21						46						71						96						121					
22						47						72						97						122					
23						48						73						98						123					
24						49						74						99						124					
25						50						75						100						125					

ANSWER SHEET

TEST NO. _____ PART _____ TITLE OF POSITION _____

(AS GIVEN IN EXAMINATION ANNOUNCEMENT - INCLUDE OPTION, IF ANY)

PLACE OF EXAMINATION _____ DATE _____

(CITY OR TOWN)   (STATE)

RATING

USE THE SPECIAL PENCIL.   MAKE GLOSSY BLACK MARKS.

	A	B	C	D	E		A	B	C	D	E		A	B	C	D	E		A	B	C	D	E		A	B	C	D	E
1						26						51						76						101					
2						27						52						77						102					
3						28						53						78						103					
4						29						54						79						104					
5						30						55						80						105					
6						31						56						81						106					
7						32						57						82						107					
8						33						58						83						108					
9						34						59						84						109					
10						35						60						85						110					

Make only ONE mark for each answer.   Additional and stray marks may be
counted as mistakes.   In making corrections, erase errors COMPLETELY.

	A	B	C	D	E		A	B	C	D	E		A	B	C	D	E		A	B	C	D	E		A	B	C	D	E
11						36						61						86						111					
12						37						62						87						112					
13						38						63						88						113					
14						39						64						89						114					
15						40						65						90						115					
16						41						66						91						116					
17						42						67						92						117					
18						43						68						93						118					
19						44						69						94						119					
20						45						70						95						120					
21						46						71						96						121					
22						47						72						97						122					
23						48						73						98						123					
24						49						74						99						124					
25						50						75						100						125					